MENTAL RETARDATION
A Programmed Manual
for Volunteer Workers

MENTAL RETARDATION
A Programmed Manual
for Volunteer Workers

By

ALDEN S. GILMORE, M.A.

Chief Psychologist, MacDonald Training Center
Assistant Professor of Research
University of South Florida
Tampa, Florida

and

THOMAS A. RICH, Ph.D., S.M. Hyg.

Professor and Chairman, Behavioral Science
University of South Florida
Tampa, Florida

With a Foreword by

MARY E. SWITZER

Commissioner
Vocational Rehabilitation Administration
Department of Health, Education, and Welfare

CHARLES C THOMAS • PUBLISHER
Springfield • Illinois • U.S.A.

Published and Distributed Throughout the World by
CHARLES C THOMAS • PUBLISHER
Bannerstone House
301-327 East Lawrence Avenue, Springfield, Illinois, U.S.A.
Natchez Plantation House
735 North Atlantic Boulevard, Fort Lauderdale, Florida, U.S.A.

© *1967, by* CHARLES C THOMAS • PUBLISHER

Library of Congress Catalog Card Number: 67-16107

With THOMAS BOOKS *careful attention is given to all details of
manufacturing and design. It is the Publisher's desire to present books
that are satisfactory as to their physical qualities and artistic possibilities
and appropriate for their particular use.* THOMAS BOOKS *will be true
to those laws of quality that assure a good name and good will.*

This investigation was supported, in part, by a research grant,
number RD-1290-P-65-C1, from the Vocational Rehabilitation Administration, Department of Health, Education, and Welfare, Washington, D. C., and may be reproduced royalty free for United States
Governmental purposes.

Printed in the United States of America
R-1

FOREWORD

In recent years public and scientific attention has been focused increasingly upon the problems of that large segment of our population, the mentally retarded. In response to pressing needs for more effective habilitation of this group, the Department of Health, Education and Welfare has vastly increased its efforts to assist in the development of new and better methods for prevention, care, treatment, and research.

The same advances in social responsibility and in the sciences which have focused our attention on the problems of the mentally retarded have created a critical scarcity of manpower, trained and capable of dealing effectively with these problems. The progress of all our combined efforts towards insuring the retarded equal opportunity for satisfying and productive lives can proceed only so fast as we are able to meet this manpower shortage. As one method for providing these services, we have come to rely more and more upon the dedicated work of the community-spirited volunteer. Without this reservoir of assistance and enthusiasm we would not have been able to make the advances we have to date.

We must, however, take upon ourselves the responsibility of providing every aid for orientation and training of this volunteer group. We must encourage the development of new knowledge and skills and favorable attitudes toward the mentally retarded.

It is for the volunteer group and for the many others facing the need for introductory training in the field of mental retardation that this manual was created. In this publication are gathered the teachings of many nationally recognized experts in the field of retardation who have worked generously in cooperation with this project. It is our sincere hope and desire that this manual will be widely utilized in the education of the volunteer and other such personnel so that we may have taken another step forward in our continuing battle to provide for the needs of the mentally retarded.

MARY E. SWITZER

Commissioner
Vocational Rehabilitation Administration
Department of Health, Education, and
    Welfare

PREFACE

This volume was written for the use of volunteer workers and others who, because of their new association with the field of mental retardation, have need for orientation and background information to aid them in preparing to work with the retarded. Early editions of the manual have proven suitable as training materials for teachers in early courses in mental retardation and special education, for institutional personnel, for in-service training of rehabilitation workers, and as ancillary aids for subprofessional workers in speech and hearing, recreation, sheltered workshop supervision and similar areas.

The information presented here is basic to any aspect of service or association with the retarded. No attempt is made to train the volunteer or other worker in a particular or specific job task. Rather, the authors have tried to provide a good informational foundation and materials which will serve as the basis for favorable attitudes toward the retarded.

The authors feel that the materials presented here and the technique by which they are presented are ideal for self instruction and adapt easily to group instruction when accompanied by supplementary materials. The technique utilized, programmed instruction, has the advantage of presenting information in logically ordered small step sequences. The manual permits the learner to proceed at his own pace and properly used provides the operant advantage of immediate feedback or knowledge of results.

The authors are indebted primarily to the Vocational Rehabilitation Administration of the Department of Health, Education, and Welfare; to the MacDonald Training Center Foundation of Tampa, Florida; and to the University of South Florida, Tampa, Florida, for the support which made this project possible. Many others have contributed generously of their time and effort. Among those who have contributed narrative materials and consultive help in preparation of this manual are:

Maxine Chambers, R.N., M.P.H., Child Development Center, University of Tennessee, Memphis, Tennessee. (Public Health)

Philip Dodge, M.D., Division of Pediatric Neurology, Massachusetts General Hospital, Boston, Massachusetts. (Pediatric Neurology)

Max Dubrow, Ph.D., Director, Association for the Help of Retarded Children, Training Center and Workshop, New York, New York. (Administration)

Norman Ellis, Ph.D., Professor of Psychology, University of Alabama, University, Alabama. (Psychology)

William Freeberg, Ph.D., Chairman, Department of Recreation, Southern Illinois University, Carbondale, Illinois. (Recreation and Outdoor Education)

Marguerite Hastings, M.S.S., Chief, Community Services for the Mentally Retarded, Department of Mental Hygiene, Baltimore, Maryland. (Social work)

Lewis B. Klebanoff, Ph.D., Consultant, Massachusetts Department of Mental Health, Boston, Massachusetts. (Community Relationships)

Leslie F. Malpass, Ph.D., Dean, College of Arts and Sciences, Virginia Polytechnic Institute, Blacksburg, Virginia. (Psychology)

Darrel J. Mase, Ph.D., Dean, College of Health Related Professions, J. Hillis Miller Health Center, University of Florida, Gainesville, Florida. (Speech)

Herbert Quay, Ph.D., Director of Research, Childrens Research Center, University of Illinois, Urbana, Illinois. (Education)

George Tarjan, M.D., Superintendent and Medical Director, Pacific State Hospital, Pomona, California. (Child Psychiatry)

Bruce Thomason, Ph.D., Chairman, Rehabilitation Counseling Program, College of Health Related Professions, University of Florida, Gainesville, Florida. (Rehabilitation)

Morton Thompson, Ph.D., Director, Consultant Service to the Ill and Handicapped, National Recreation Association, New York, New York. (Recreation)

Clarence Webb, Ph.D., Associate Professor of Behavioral Science, Director, Communication Disorders Training Program, University of South Florida, Tampa, Florida. (Speech)

As is necessary in programmed instruction, trial application of programmed sequences was used to assure effective presentation of materials, interest level, and adequate communication of both information and attitudes. We are grateful to Maurice Dayan, Ph.D., Director of Research and Training, Pinecrest State School, Pineville, Louisiana, who assisted in trial applications of the manual with cottage parents in on-the-job training; to William Price, L.L.B., and Gerald Eaglen, M.A., both of the University of Southern Illinois, who cooperated in trial application of the manual with a training group of recreation workers and volunteers at the Little Grassy Facility of Southern Illinois University; to the Junior League of St. Petersburg and Tampa, Florida; and to the many other local service groups and individuals who acted as subjects in trial presentations.

Calvin M. Pinkard, Jr., Ph.D. and Lawrence H. Ricker, Ph.D., Co-directors of Research of the MacDonald Training Center, Research and Education Division, were most helpful in providing assistance and a favorable research climate. Special recognition is due to Charles F. Williams, M.S. Research Psychologist and Chief Programmer of the

MacDonald Training Center, Research and Education Division, Tampa, Florida, and to Margaret P. Hunnicutt, B.A., both of whom held major responsibility for programming much of the narrative material. Also due recognition are Richard Bothwell, of the *St. Petersburg Times*, St. Petersburg, Florida, artist for the project, and Barbara Sparkman, Research Assistant and Secretary.

ALDEN S. GILMORE
THOMAS A. RICH

CONTENTS

MENTAL RETARDATION
A Programmed Manual
for Volunteer Workers

PROGRAMMED INSTRUCTION?

Most of us are inclined to approach printed matter as if it were a novel. When we pick up a technical book we try to read at the same rate of speed as we would in reading for entertainment. We frequently scan over paragraphs and even pages without really knowing what we have been reading. Even though we have all experienced this many times, we still like to feel that information can somehow be absorbed magically merely by being exposed to it. When we find that we are not able to absorb the information at our

3

usual reading speed, then we hear the complaint of dull-dry reading material.

Much of the content of this manual will look different to you because it is broken down into small bits of information. Many of the sentences will ask that you fill in missing words. The object is not to test you on the information, but to help you concentrate on the material and avoid the general pattern of reading too rapidly with the risk of not absorbing essential details.

One of the main objects of this style "programmed learning" is to involve the reader in actual participation rather than just passive reading. If, as you read, you find you are missing answers you may be trying to proceed too rapidly. Although your reading speed will be much slower, please keep in mind that in "programmed" form, the amount of material is much less than if the same subject matter were presented in textbook form. Programmed material tends to concentrate more on basic concepts. Programmed material also permits you to proceed at your own rate of speed.

When you have to fill in a blank, just go ahead and write in the answer or at least decide on what the answer should be before you go to the next item. Remember, you'll know right away whether you're right or wrong, so you won't have a chance to build on, or develop habits based on misinformation; and most of the time, your answer will be right.

Let's see how "programming" works. Take a 4 x 6 file card or a folded sheet of paper and cover up Item 2 on page 6 (see illustration below).

Read Item 1, decide on an answer, then slide the card down to expose Item 2. The answer to Item 1 is to the left of Item 2. (In this case, the answer is "Mental Retardation.")

Next read Item 2, decide on an answer, and slide your cover sheet down to check your answer.

	1. This booklet is about the general subject of men_____ ret_____ .
mental retardation	2. That wasn't too_____, was it?
hard, difficult	3. The first step in preparing this manual was a national and local survey to find out what the volunteer _____ to know about retardation.
wanted	4. You probably filled in the above blank with the word "needed." There may be some difference between exactly what volunteers *need* to know and what they _____ to know about retardation.
want	5. This is an important difference because a person will pay much more_____ to information he *wants* to know.
attention	6. The second step in planning for this manual was to find the best method of _____ this material to volunteers.
presenting	7. Research has shown that programmed learning is one of the fastest and most _____ methods of teaching.
effective	8. In the exercise which you are now doing, we are leaving certain words out of each sentence in order to concentrate your _____ upon important words.
attention	9. You will see that most of the words we asked you to fill in are the key_____

	we are trying to communicate.
words	10. Many people have asked, "What if I fill in the blank with a word which is _____ from the answer below? Is this an error?"
different	11. No. Frequently people will use a synonym instead of the _____ given. this is perfectly all right.
answer, word	12. Please remember, although programmed material may look like a test it is not intended to be a _____.
test	13. In most cases the answers will just come _____, and you'll remember them longer.
naturally	14. Now, would you like to prove to yourself the difference between programmed instruction and regular text material in paragraph form? If so, stop right now and see how much you can remember from the first printed page as compared with the past thirteen frames of programming.
	15. Did you stop and try to recall the first page of material or did you just keep on to this frame? Remember, if you want to learn effectively from this material you must _____ your answer each time before you move your card down the page.
write	16. Any kind of learning requires some work

	on your part. You may look back but try not to look ———————.
ahead	17. Now you should be ready to start on the first section. Have ———————!
fun	

MENTAL RETARDATION -

AN INTRODUCTION

9

	1. A mentally retarded person is a slow person—*slow* to develop, *slow* to learn, and _____ to adjust to society.
slow	2. If he is just slow, you wonder, why can't he simply catch up? A mental retardate cannot "catch up" because he is not only _____ but he is also *limited* in ability.
slow	3. Being slow and _____ in ability does not mean, though, that he cannot be taught many useful things.
limited	4. Although all retardates are slow and limited in ability, they are not all _____ and _____ to the same degree.
slow limited	5. There are many _____ of mental retardation.
degrees, levels	6. Those who are severely _____ are unable to learn anything but the most basic self-care skills.
retarded	7. Those who are mildly retarded are able to learn so much that as adults some are no longer identified as being _____.
retarded	8. Many others fall in the wide range between the s_____ and m_____ retarded.
severely mildly	9. Later you will learn more about degrees of mental retardation but for now let's talk a little about what causes retardation.

	10. A mentally retarded person is what he is because of something that happened before his birth, or during his birth, or early in his _____.
childhood	11. No one knows all the causes of mental retardation. More than 100 have been identified and many others have been suspected. If you will look at the chart (on page 12) you will see that these causes fall into five major categories.
	12. If you find you need help in reading the following frames refer to the chart.
	13. Retardation can be the result of an incompatibility of _____ inherited from the mother and father.
genes	14. One example of how retardation can stem from genetic inheritance is a condition called PKU.
	15. PKU stands for phenylketonuria (you can see why it's commonly abbreviated).
	16. Although PKU occurs only once in about 30,000 births it is a dramatic example of how medical science can actually prevent mental _____. For this reason PKU has received wide publicity.
retardation	17. Before a new born infant leaves the hospital, a simple blood test can detect _____ and the retardation which would develop can be prevented by dietary control.

CAUSES OF RETARDATION

GENETIC IRREGULARITIES	1. Inheritance of genes which produce poor intellectual functioning. 2. Disorders of the genes caused by over exposure to X-ray, infections, etc. 3. Recessive genetic trait which produces an error in metabolism producing mental retardation (for example, PKU). 4. RH blood factor incompatibility. 5. Mongolism resulting from extra chromosome.
DURING PREGNANCY	1. German measles. 2. Glandular disorders. 3. Poisons, tumors, infections. 4. Poor nutrition.
AT BIRTH	1. Prolonged labor. 2. Too rapid birth. 3. Premature birth. 4. Any circumstance that reduces oxygen supply to infant's brain.
AFTER BIRTH	1. Childhood diseases as whooping cough, chicken pox, measles, meningitis, scarlet fever, polio, encephalitis. (Especially in very young.) 2. Glandular imbalance. 3. Severe injuries to the brain. 4. Lack of certain chemicals in blood.
ENVIRONMENTAL FACTORS	1. Educational deprivation. 2. Serious emotional problems.

PKU	18. Retardation can be caused by common German _____ or by_____ disorders during pregnancy.
measles glandular	19. Retardation can be the result of any circumstance that reduces the _____ supply to the infant's brain.
oxygen	20. Retardation can be the result of prolonged_____ , obstetrical complications, _____ birth, or a too rapid birth process.
labor premature	21. Retardation can be caused by some childhood _____ or _____ imbalance.
diseases glandular	22. Prevention of normal digestion due to lack of certain _____ in the blood can cause retardation.
chemicals	23. Still another factor causing retardation can be damage to the_____through an accident or high fever.
brain	24. Such a child would be referred to as _____damaged or brain-injured. The technical term is "neurological damage."
brain-	25. Up to this point we have dealt with specific physical causes of retardation. Yet by far the largest group of the mentally retarded is made of individuals who show no definite _____ cause for being retarded. They are usually classified as being mildly mentally retarded.

| physical | 26. A large number of these individuals are born and reared in deprived environments where there is little opportunity to learn. |

	27. Retardation can be the result of a lack of opportunity to_____early in life.
learn	28. One who is retarded because of the lack of opportunity to learn early in life is said to be culturally_____.
retarded	29. Retardation can also be caused by serious *emotional* problems early in life.
	30. Normal intellectual development does not occur when a child suffers continued and serious_____ problems.

emotional	31. You might wonder how you can tell a mentally retarded child from a normal child. Can you tell by looking at him?
no	32. Most of the retarded *(do/do not)* look different from normal children but differ only in their ability to learn.
do not	33. However, there are some *clinical* types of retardation in which the retarded child will differ from a normal child in physical appearance.
	34. Mongoloids, cretins, and microcephalics are examples of _____ types.
clinical	35. You will seldom find a retardate who does not also have some _____ handicaps.
physical	36. Speech, visual and hearing defects, cerebral palsy, and epilepsy are some physical _____ common among the retarded.
handicaps	37. It is important to remember that although these handicaps are common among the retarded this does *not* mean that people who suffer from these physical handicaps are necessarily mentally retarded.
	38. As well as physical _____, emotional disturbances are also common among the retarded.
handicaps	39. Because most retardates know that they

	are _____ from normal children, it is important to let them know that you like and appreciate them for themselves.
different	40. Another characteristic of the retarded is the _____ and _____ development of physical skills.

slow limited	41. It is commonly thought that retardates make up for their lack of mental ability by being able to work well with their _____ .
hands	42. Many people think that because the

	retarded cannot handle jobs that require much _____ that they would make good assembly line workers.
intelligence, reasoning	43. Remember that all retarded are slow and limited not only in mental development but also in the development of _____ skills.
physical	44. According to their mental ages, retardates are usually classified as belonging to one of three groups.
	45. The first group is made up of the *mildly* _____ who are called *educables*.
retarded	46. These mildly retarded or _____ can learn approximately to sixth grade level but progress slowly in school.
educables	47. As adults, _____ retardates can hold simple jobs and possibly live independently.
educable	48. The second group is made up of the *moderately* _____ who are called *trainables*.
retarded	49. The moderately retarded or _____ cannot learn academic subjects in school.
trainables	50. As adults, _____ retardates will never be independent and the most they will be able to do is perform simple tasks in sheltered settings.
trainable	51. The third group is made up of the *severely*

and *profoundly*_____.

retarded	52. The retarded who require lifelong care and supervision and are often confined to mental institutions are referred to as _____ and _____ retarded.
severely profoundly	53. The purpose of this manual is to help the volunteer understand the *mildly* retarded "ed_____" and the *moderately* retarded "tr_____."
educables trainables	54. It is often thought that it takes a certain kind of person to work with the retarded, but _____who is patient and kind can successfully do so.
anyone	55. Many people would like to help retarded children but feel that it is_____ in most cases.
hopeless	56. Although retardates are_____ and _____in learning, educable and trainable retardates can be taught many useful things.

slow limited	57. As a _____ you can contribute a great deal to the happiness and accomplishments of the retarded.
volunteer	58. You might help by working in a clinic, hospital, sheltered workshop, school, special class, or recreational program.
	59. As a volunteer there are many things that you will need and want to know about _____ people in general.
retarded	60. A mentally _____ person is often a shy, lonely, and isolated person.
retarded	61. He is not as good at making _____ and getting along well in his group as others are.
friends	62. A retarded person frequently loses jobs because of his _____ to get along with people.
inability	63. As a volunteer you can be the understanding _____ who likes him for what he is.
friend	64. Your understanding will help him realize that there are many other people in the world with whom he can be _____.
friends	65. Remember in working with a retarded person that words do not mean as much to him as they do to you. Telling him how to do a thing does not help him as much as _____ him.

showing	66. If instructions are necessary give them step by step and in simple _____.
words	67. He will learn more easily if he can start with a task he can _____.
accomplish do	68. After that he should be helped to progress by one _____ at a time.
step	69. He will make many mistakes but each time he succeeds he should be _____.
praised	70. The best motivation for the retarded is encouragement and _____.
praise	71. However, your _____ should be directed toward improvement so that the child can progress.
encouragement	72. As with normal children, the retarded should be held to some degree of _____.
achievement	73. Does the retardate have a sense of humor? He does, but humor must be geared to his _____ of mentality.
level	74. Many retarded are hindered by not being able to express themselves. Helping the retarded learn to _____ himself will be an important task for the volunteer.

express	75. As a volunteer you can accomplish a great deal with the retarded in most cases, but problems will arise at times which will require help of professional people.
	76. Rather than try to solve a difficult problem alone, it is better for the volunteer to seek _____ help early.
professional	

EDUCATION

	1. You have learned two terms that are commonly used to describe levels of retardation. The *mildly retarded* who can learn to approximately _____ grade level and who can eventually live _____ are called _____ retardates.
sixth independently educable	2. The *moderately retarded* who cannot learn _____ subjects, who will always need care and _____, and who can perform only simple _____ in _____ settings, are called _____ retardates.

academic supervision tasks sheltered trainable	3. If you had no difficulty with the above frames, have a cup of coffee and proceed to Frame 13.
	4. Understanding the difference between the two terms "ed_____" and "tr_____" will be very useful to you.
educable trainable	5. These terms will give you an indication of how much a retardate will usually be able to _____ .
learn	6. The *mildly retarded* with mental ages ranging from eight to twelve are called _____ retardates.
educable	7. The *moderately retarded* with mental ages ranging from five to eight are called _____ retardates.
trainable	8. A retardate who can learn simple academic subjects such as reading, writing and arithmetic, to approximately sixth grade level, would be called an _____ retardate.
educable	9. A retardate who cannot learn academic subjects would be called a _____ retardate.
trainable	10. As adults, _____ retardates can hold simple jobs and possibly live independently.

educable	11. As adults,_____ retardates will rarely be independent and the most they will be able to do is perform simple tasks in sheltered settings.
trainable	12. In working with trainables remember that they are slower to learn and more limited in ability than _____ .
educables	13. There are approximately *five times more educable retardates* than slower learning _____ retardates.

TRAINABLES

trainable	14. In the section that follows you will learn more about educable retardates—their capabilities and their limitations—but for now let's concentrate on the _____ learning trainables.
slower	15. Trainables will usually not profit from a regular type school program since they cannot learn _____ subjects.
academic	16. For this reason many communities have "special" classes or even entire schools for teaching _____ retardates.
trainable	17. Trainables usually attend _____ classes or schools where they are taught basic skills such as *self-care* and *speech*.
special	18. However, when they reach age sixteen in most communities they are no longer eligible for public school education. At this point most of them will have a mental age ranging from five to eight years and will still require care and _____ .
supervision	19. Besides special schools, many communities have sheltered workshops. Shops in which the retarded can work at simple _____ under close supervision are called sheltered workshops.
tasks, jobs	20. Although they can learn only basic skills, some trainables will be able

	to do simple tasks at home or in a _____ _____ .
sheltered workshop	21. Usually all that you can expect of trainable retardates is that they develop self-care skills, be able to carry on simple conversations, and perform simple _____ .
tasks	22. There are many things you can do to help trainable retardates learn and develop. You might begin by helping them learn self-_____ skills such as dressing, toileting, and eating.
care	23. Remember that all retardates learn slowly. Trainables will require much *drill* and *practice* in developing _____ _____ skills.
self-care	24. Learning to button a coat, to use a toothbrush, to eat with a spoon—all of these simple things will require much drill and _____ .
practice	25. Praise and enc_____ are very good motivations for learning.
encourage-ment	26. When a trainable retardate tries but fails to perform a task he should not be _____ .
criticized, made fun of, ridiculed	27. The volunteer should _____ and encourage each small accomplishment and avoid _____ for failure.
praise criticism	28. Another way to assist is to encourage *speech* in the retardate. Many use

	gestures rather than words. By pretending not to understand gestures you can encourage them to use _____ .
speech	29. Like normal children, some retardates are timid, and getting them to talk will be a _____ process. Family, a favorite subject of children, provides an easy way to start conversation.
slow, hard	30. These conversations give an excellent opportunity to help the retardate in the development of his _____ .
speech	31. It will also lead to a better _____ of each child.
under-standing	32. Ability to speak and to understand what others are saying is very important if trainable retardates are to perform simple tasks in a _____ or at _____ .
workshop home	33. Another thing the trainable must be taught is to _____ common hazards and dangers.
avoid, recognize	34. Watching for cars when crossing a street, not touching a hot stove in the kitchen—all these simple things must be _____ .
taught	35. With constant repetition they will eventually learn to avoid common hazards and _____ .
dangers	36. Remember that what a normal child

		grasps quickly must be patiently _____to a trainable retardate.
taught	37.	It may seem that the trainable retardate will accomplish very little over a long period of time, but to the trainable each small _____is very important.
success, accomplish- ment		

EDUCABLES

	38. Earlier in this section we found that there are about five times more _____ retarded than there are trainable retarded.
educable	39. Retardates with mental ages ranging from eight to twelve are called _____ retardates.
educable	40. Retardates who are able to do the work in grades three to seven are called _____ retardates.
educable	41. But more important than actual mental age or grade level, the _____ retardate should be able to learn skills which will allow him eventually to hold a simple job and live independently.
educable	42. This ability to live independently is the main difference which separates educables from _____ .
trainables	43. Educables must be taught many practical things including reading, writing, and arithmetic, if they are to live _____ _____ .
independently	44. Educables usually attend regular school classes while in the _____ grades.
primary, early, lower	45. However, during the first and second grades they will usually fall _____ their school mates.
behind	46. A few educables might reach as high as

_____ grade level before leaving school at sixteen.

seventh	47. In most cases educables will remain between _____ and fifth grade level in their learning.

third	48. Educables have more trouble with abstract kinds of learning than with more practical, concrete kinds of _____.
learning	49. Reasoning and figuring out problems are types of _____ learning.
abstract	50. Reading comprehension and arithmetic reasoning are forms of _____ learning.
abstract	51. Rote learning such as memorizing is a

		form of _____ learning.
concrete	52.	Spelling, counting, and learning number facts are forms of _____ learning.
concrete	53.	Most educables are able to learn simple addition and _____ .
subtraction	54.	A few educables will be able to proceed to _____ arithmetic problems.
simple	55.	Arithmetic instruction should stress the solving of *practical* problems since _____can learn skills enabling them to hold simple jobs.
educables	56.	One of the most practical things they will learn is the handling of _____ ($).
money	57.	Understanding common measurements will be necessary for many of the _____ available to them.
jobs	58.	Being able to tell the _____ of day is important and also brings them much self-satisfaction.
time	59.	Learning simple arithmetic facts will also help them in their _____ and daily living.
jobs	60.	Educable retardates are limited in their ability to reason. It is hard for them to generalize or _____ what they have learned to another set of circumstances.

transfer, apply	61. Because their ability to reason is _____, much drill and practice are necessary for them to learn arithmetic.
limited	62. Drill and _____ help promote learning.
practice	63. Reward and praise for even small accomplishments also help promote _____.
learning	64. *Language* and *communication skills* are particularly hard even for _ed_____ retardates.
educable	65. Being able to understand what others are saying and being able to express their own _____ will be very important in their daily living.
ideas, thoughts	66. Educables can be taught to carry on ordinary _conv_____.
conver-sations	67. They usually cannot be taught to read and _____ past the fifth grade level.
write	68. Some educables may be able to recognize only ten or twenty words even after _____ of schooling.
years	69. Most educables, however, will learn to recognize several hundred words and be able to _____ first and second grade books.

read	70. One reason language and communication skills are difficult for them is that they do not have good voc_____.
vocabu- laries	71. Another reason is that they are not able to associate or_____ ideas.
connect	72. There are many ways to help educable retardates develop language_____.
skills	73. Many retarded children have been under-privileged. They have not been encouraged to learn or given opportunities to _____.
learn	74. One way to provide them with opportunities to learn is by reading them interesting_____ at their level.
books, stories	75. Reading to them and showing them pictures will enc_____ them to look at books.

encourage	76. Remember to _____ them to relate their own experiences and tell stories.
encourage	77. Responding to *verbal* commands and solving *verbal* problems also helps them develop _____ skills.
language	78. A good way to provide them with drill and practice is by playing games in which the children must obey_____ commands.

verbal, spoken	79. Another way of providing them with opportunities to learn is through *field trips*. Volunteers can be helpful by chaperoning field_____.
trips	80. Educables can learn many practical things through _____ _____ , for example, getting around on a city bus.
field trips	81. Remember that educables are able to develop skills for living _____.

independ- ently	82. About 80 per cent of educable retardates are able to become self-_____.
supporting	83. Because many of them will marry and have children, it is important that the girls develop skills in homemaking. Such _____ skills as child care, cooking, cleaning, mending, and purchasing are important.
home- making	84. Teaching homemaking skills can be one of the most important contributions of the _____.
volunteer	85. Both boys and girls should be taught skills that will help them get and hold _____.
jobs	86. The jobs most commonly held by educable retardates are in the *service* occupations.
	87. Food preparation, laundry and cleaning, janitorial service, and housekeeping are forms of _____ occupations.
service	88. Vocational training in _____ occupations can be contributed by volunteers.
service	89. In order to get and hold jobs it is important that they learn good work _____.
habits	90. It is also important that they learn social skills. Many of the retarded lose jobs because of their _____ to get along well with others.

inability	91. Most important is good character development. If they are to stay out of trouble, rules of good _____ must be learned and practiced by them.
conduct, behavior	92. The retarded are capable of understanding discipline. They must be taught right from _____.
wrong	93. They must be taught to separate that which is permitted from that which is _____.
forbidden, not permitted	94. In helping them to learn discipline, being firm yet kind is better than scolding and _____.
criticizing	95. Leisure time can become a problem if they are not taught to spend it in acceptable ways. Interest in hobbies will give them an acceptable way to fill their _____ time.
leisure, spare	96. The volunteer can be very helpful in teaching arts and crafts which will help lead retardates to enjoyable _____.
hobbies	97. Volunteers might make special contributions through teaching the retarded their own _____.
hobbies	

BEHAVIOR

In this section we are going to discuss the potential of the retarded child, behavioral expectations, his emotional needs, strengths and weaknesses, and how to motivate the child toward improved adaptive behavior.

There are two terms commonly used in discussion of the mentally retarded, both of which you should understand before getting into this section.

1. The first term is "*adaptive behavior*" which means *the way we cope with the*

natural and social demands of our environment.

2. Adaptive_____is usually measured in terms of:
   (1) the degree to which the person
meets the standards of "personal inde-
pendence" expected of his age, and
   (2) the degree to which the person
meets the standards of "social responsibility" expected of his age.

behavior

3. What is meant by "personal indepen-
dence?" Just this: has the person developed the self-_____skills and
motor _____ he needs to function and maintain himself independently?

care
abilities

4. By "social responsibility" we mean:
How well does he get along with others?
Is he reliable? Trustworthy? And is he
able to strive for a long-range goal in-
stead of thinking only in terms of immediate pleasures?

5. Adaptive behavior is usually measured
in terms of personal _____
and social _____ .

indepen-
dence
responsi-
bility

6. From this we can see that the mentally
retarded person usually shows a low
measure of _____ behavior from
birth or early _____ .

adaptive
childhood

7. He __is/is not__ able to cope with his
environment in a way that we view as
normal.

is not	8. The behavior of the mentally retarded person is usually not adequate for his _____ .
environ-ment	9. Should we judge his behavior though, without considering how complex his environment is? A person viewed as mentally retarded in a large city might not be viewed as_____on a farm.
retarded	10. His behavior in the city may be inadequate, but his behavior on the farm may be quite_____and be seen by most people as normal.
adequate	11. So we can't judge behavior without con-

considering the _____ where it occurs.

environ-ment	12. Our task may involve changing the _____ of the retarded person, making it simpler. An extreme might be to place him in an institution where demands on him are few.
environ-ment	13. Or our task may involve changing the _____ of the person, that is, teaching skills which may permit him to adapt more easily.
behavior	14. Sometimes we may be called on to do both—simplify the _____ so that he can adjust to it, and make the person's _____ more adequate.
environ-ment	15. Most of us think of the home _____ _____ as a simple or sheltered one

behavior	but for the more severely or profoundly retarded, it can be quite complex.
environment	16. Using knives, forks, and spoons seems a simple task to a normal person, but for a retarded person with a mental age of three using knives, forks, and spoons may be a very_____task.

difficult, complex	17. Remember that the_____of the environment depends upon the person viewing it.
complexity, difficulty	18. We must be careful that we do not view the world from the standpoint of our own abilities when considering it for the _____ person.
retarded	19. Now we are ready for the second term, "I.Q." This is a term used by almost everyone but not everyone knows exactly what I.Q. is or how it is determined.
	20. I.Q. is the degree to which a person's level of performance is below or _____ that typical of his age group.

above	21. I.Q. stands for intelligence quotient —the mental age divided by the chronological age.
	22. Chronological ____ is the person's actual age.
age	23. Mental _____ is the level at which a person performs. Mental age can be determined in many ways. One way is through intelligence tests.
age	24. A boy whose actual age is ten may perform like an average twelve year old on an intelligence test, thus his _____ _____ is twelve years.
mental age	25. No matter what his chronological age, if he performs like an average twelve year old, his mental age is _____ years.
twelve	26. Now that you know that chronological age is simply the person's _____ age and that mental age is the age level at which he _____, here is the formula for arriving at I.Q.: $$I.Q. = \frac{MA\ (mental\ age)}{CA\ (chronological\ age)} \times 100$$

	Multiplying by 100 just makes the figure easier to read because it takes away the decimal point.
actual performs	27. Using this formula, what is the I.Q. of a sixteen year old boy whose intelligence test shows that he performs like an average eight year old?
50	28. You are right. His I.Q. is 50. $$I.Q. = \frac{8}{16} = .5 \times 100 = 50$$
	29. The term "I.Q." has enjoyed such popularity over the past years that people are often prone to overemphasize it. This relationship between age and mental functioning is but one of many things that go into making a person what he is, and should not be given the significance that is so often attributed to it by popular magazines, TV, etc.

DEGREE OF MENTAL RETARDATION

Descriptive Term	Intelligence Quotient Approximate I.Q. Ranges
Profound	Below 20
Severe	20 - 35
Moderate (Trainable)	36 - 50
Mild (Educable)	51 - 80

POTENTIAL OF THE RETARDED CHILD

	30. All of the mentally retarded have potential for improvement.
	31. A common misconception is that only the educable or trainable retardate has such _____ .
potential	32. With an I.Q. of 50 to 75 or so, the _____ retardate can be taught some academic skills, and social skills, and may frequently be prepared for employment.
educable	33. With an I.Q. of 25 or 50, the _____ retardate can be taught many of these skills to a lesser degree.
trainable	34. But what about the retarded with I.Q.s of less than 25, those who are considered _____ and _____ retarded?
severely profoundly	35. The severely retarded person who has not even developed self-care _____ is often viewed as "untrainable" or "hopeless."
skills	36. Let's consider a child who is not toilet trained, cannot feed himself, dress or bathe himself—who has no _____ skills.
self-care	37. Suppose through training we are able to teach this child to do some of these tasks for himself?

	38. The proportionate gain for the severely retarded child would actually be greater than the gain for the educable child who made similar progress.
	39. Such a child, of course, can't usually be trained to the extent that he could attend school or sheltered workshops but will always remain in the_____ or in an institution.
home	40. Consider the fantastic cost of maintaining a person for fifty or sixty years who requires that all his _____ be met by others.
needs	41. Consider also the cost to the person in terms of human dignity in being completely helpless and dependent upon others.
	42. All mentally retarded children have _____ for some growth and improvement.
potential	43. Research has shown that even the most retarded child has potential and that no retarded child should be viewed as _____.

BEHAVIORAL EXPECTATIONS

hopeless	44. We must keep in mind, though, the extent of the retarded person's_____

when we set standards for his behavior.

potential	45. Although we have been warned against it, too often we expect our children, normal or retarded, to act like "little _____."
adults	46. The normal child, gradually but eventually, does take on the behavior of an _____, acquiring new mental and physical abilities as he grows older.
adult	47. But the retarded child, even one who is but mildly retarded, advances only to the mental level of a _____ or _____ year old normal child.
ten or twelve	48. He may not advance past the level of a nine month old baby if he is _____ retarded.
severely	49. Although many times the physical body of such a child can be trained past the level of nine months, his _____ ability will still be that of a baby.
mental	50. Yet, we attempt to teach these "children" skills and_____ graces that will make them more like normal adults.
social	51. We expect them to eat with the proper utensils, cope with toys designed for _____children, and so on.
normal	52. We are too often bound by our own adult _____ in our training of the retarded.

standards	53. In other words, we expect them to react to an _____ designed for normal adults or normal children.
environ- ment	54. A newcomer to the field of mental retar- dation may be deceived into expecting the retardate to _____ in a manner beyond his means.
behave	55. In our society we learn that small people behave like children and large people behave like _____.
adults	56. It is hard to realize sometimes that the retardate's physical size is not in keep- ing with his _____ ability.

mental	57. We may find a teenage retardate of normal physical size and yet with the _____ capacity of a three year old child.
mental	58. It is very difficult to overcome the feel- ing that there is a relationship between

size and _____ even for professionals in the field.

ability	59.	The volunteer must constantly remind himself that this person is going to be childlike and that his behavior, including his judgment, reasoning, abstract thinking, social graces, and even his physical skills, will not be in _____ _____ to his size.
proportion, relation		

MOTIVATION

	60.	How can we help the retarded child move toward improved adaptive _____?
behavior	61.	Like all of us, the retarded child must be *motivated* in order to learn and develop.
	62.	Another word for "urge," "drive," or "push" is _____ .
motivation	63.	Among retarded children, as among the normal, we see all degrees of _____ _____ .
motivation	64.	Some seem lazy and others seem "bursting" to be at various activities.
	65.	We should not view the seemingly lazy child simply as one who lacks the intelligence to respond to his _____ .

environ- ment	66. Instead, he may be a child whose past responses were unrewarded. The retarded are best ＿＿＿＿＿＿by reward and encouragement.
motivated	67. A child who is not ＿＿＿＿＿＿for his responses may cease to respond and appear lazy.
rewarded	68. Retarded children must be motivated to join in recreational, social, and other activities and when they do, they must receive ＿＿＿＿＿＿.
rewards, encourage- ment	69. Sometimes institutions are set up in a way that is not conducive to establishing motivation.
	70. Generally an institution gives the child everything he needs including those things which the normal child must usually ＿＿＿＿＿ for.

work	71. The policy of meeting all a child's needs whether or not he puts forth_____ often produces behavioral problems and seemingly unmotivated, listless people.
effort	72. Society does not work this way. The normal person usually is rewarded only when he has_____a reward.
earned	73. Programs for the retarded should include the "work for" or "reward" principle.
	74. However, the behavior required to earn rewards should be in keeping with the retarded person's_____.
potential, ability	75. Regular brushing of teeth, dressing, helping another patient, etc., are examples of behavior that could be_____.
rewarded	76. Later we will see how affection can be used as a reward to _____ the retarded.
motivate	77. Other rewards might be special privileges, foods, entertainment, and the many rewards we use to _____ normal children.
motivate	78. Volunteer workers with the retarded often can adopt this principle of "_____ for" a reward.
work	79. Every child needs affection from an adult. The retarded child wants and needs _____just as a normal child does.

affection	80. If you have ever visited an institution you were probably struck by the way many of the children crowded around and responded to visitors in an _____way.

affection-ate	81. In institutions, children are often kept in large groups, typically with only two or three substitute parents or attendants for thirty or more children.
	82. Under these circumstances it is hard for the child to develop the_____ relationship he needs with an adult.

affec- tionate	83. The volunteer who serves in an institu- tion can render an especially important service in this respect.
	84. Many children in institutions seem to be withdrawn and to show little interest in their _____.
environ- ment, surround- ings	85. This may not be due entirely to low intelligence but may in part be due to the fact that in the past the child has not been _____ for responding to his environment or to people.
rewarded	86. The need for affection can be the most valuable "tool" we have for leading the retarded toward more _____ be- havior.
adaptive	87. Affection can be used as a _____ , motivating a child to do many things for himself.
reward	88. This doesn't mean you should not be warm and accepting at all times, but it does mean that special attention should be used as a _____ .
reward	89. The more response a child shows to his surroundings the more apt he is to _____.
learn, develop	90. The sooner you can develop emotional _____ in the withdrawn child, the sooner he will begin to learn.

responses	91. The important thing to remember is that just because a child doesn't express his need for _____doesn't mean the need is not there.
affection	

STRENGTHS AND WEAKNESSES OF THE RETARDED

	92. Throughout the modern era both the parent and professional have tried to strengthen the very characteristic which is weakest in the retarded, that is their mental ability.
	93. Teaching techniques seem to have stressed concentration on the_____ of the retarded.
weak- nesses	94. For example, a teacher will concentrate on a child's reading if this is his greatest _____ .
weakness	95. Such an approach may not only be mean-ingless but may lead to failure, frustra-tion, discouragement, and unacceptable _____ .
behavior	96. No child should be permitted to meet with_____ *too* often.
failure	97. Often when the teacher tries to strengthen weaknesses the child meets with_____ .

failure	98.	This is not to say the child should be limited to *only* those things at which he can _____.
succeed	99.	Try to find the middle ground. Don't do for him what he can do, but support him until he learns to do those things he has the _____ to do.
ability	100.	Training for the retarded should consist of a mixture of those things he is "good at" and those he has difficulty with, but make sure he _____ more often than he _____.
succeeds fails	101.	It is as true for the retarded as it is for each of us, that success, not failure, encourages us to strive for the next goal.

PHYSICAL ABILITY

- Is there a relationship between physical ability and mental ability?
- Do retarded children develop physical skills at the same rate as normal children?
- Can a trainable retardate learn complicated physical tasks?
- Do most retarded children eventually catch up with normal children in physical skills?
- What can I do?

	1. The development of adequate _____ skills is very important for retarded children because this may be one of their greatest assets later in life.

physical	2. We are all so familiar with the words ''physical skill'' that we seldom think about them in a *technical* way. The phrase ''motor ability'' is a more _____ term for physical skill.
technical, precise	3. Motor ability has to do with how well a child can control the movements of different parts of his _____ .
body	4. As a volunteer, your services will be of value just helping out in classroom or recreational activities. Your contribution can be even greater if you know more about _____ ability.
motor	5. Motor ability can be broken down into four major parts: (1) coordination, (2) accuracy, (3) speed, and (4) strength.
	6. It isn't ordinarily true that a child is uniformly good or poor in all of these four different kinds of motor ability. For example, a child may be strong for his age but have poor_____ .
coordina-tion	7. He may have enough speed but lack acc_____ .
accuracy	8. An awareness of these different kinds of_____ skills will help you recognize and assist with individual problems.
motor	9. Let's review! The four kinds of motor

	skills are: (1)————— (2)————, (3)—————, and (4)————— .
accuracy speed coordina- tion strength	10. There is a great deal of overlap between these different kinds of motor control. Throwing a baseball may seem simple but it is a complex physical skill involving not only coordination but———, —————, and ————— .
speed accuracy strength	11. In addition to these four major categories of motor ability, two other terms are important to know: "agility" and "endurance."
	12. Agility refers to the ability to change or adapt to new situations. Basketball is a game which requires a great deal of ————— .
agility	13. The word "endurance" means reserve strength, or the ability to keep at a task. A retarded child who may appear to have normal strength may have very little ————— .
endurance	14. It is quite common for trainable children to have very little endurance. They may become exhausted very————.
easily, quickly	15. A good recreation program will have activities that give practice in each of these kinds of ————— skills.
motor	16. A recreation or physical education program will be more effective if records of each child's ————— are kept.

progress, ability, perform- ance	17. Most retarded children progress very slowly and small changes may not be _____ by the volunteer or by the child himself.
seen, recognized, noticed	18. The volunteer should try to be aware of small changes in each child's development in coordination, accuracy, _____ , and _____ .
speed strength	19. Keeping records of each child's ability to lift weights would be a measure of _____ .
strength	20. Keeping time records of running fifty yards would measure _____ .
speed	21. The ability to balance on one foot would be a measure of _____ .
coordina- tion	22. Knot-tying is a good example of _____ _____ .
coordina-	23. Dart-throwing involves a lot of coordination but is also a good test of _____ .

accuracy	24. A large number of tests are available to evaluate_____ abilities. The aid of a professional person in physical education can usually be enlisted to set up a physical development program.
motor	25. Now, let's go back to the questions at the beginning of this section. Is there a relationship between physical ability and mental ability? Yes_____ No_____
yes	26. Coordination, accuracy, and speed do show a relationship to mental ability. This would suggest that most trainable children have_____ motor skill than educable children.
less	27. It follows that many educable children may have_____ motor skill than normal children.
less	28. Do retarded children develop physical abilities at the same rate as normal children? Yes_____ No_____
no	29. However, retarded children follow the same pattern of development as normal children in learning to sit, stand, walk, etc., although they are often much _____ than normal children in developing these abilities which require motor control.
slower	30. Do retarded children eventually catch up with normal children in developing these abilities which require motor control? Yes_____ No_____

no	31. Most people would answer "yes" to this question but actually the majority of retarded children tend to fall more and more behind normal children and never catch up.
	32. In all of these statements remember that there are many "_____ to the rule."
exceptions	33. Can a trainable retarded child usually learn complex tasks? Yes_____ No_____
no	34. With much practice trainable children can learn to do many things, but very few can master the complex physical tasks needed to obtain employment.
	35. Can educable children learn complex physical tasks? Yes _____ No _____
yes	36. Most educable children can be taught to perform complex motor tasks, such as routine machine operation.

	37. Usually a great deal of training and prac_____ are required for educable retarded persons to learn highly complex tasks but it can be done.
practice	38. What can I do? By being aware of the factor of motor ability and how it differs with retarded children, you can help them develop specific aspects of motor control rather than just supervising games.
	39. A great deal of patience, practice, and encouragement is required in many cases to achieve even small progress. But a number of research studies show that retarded children can show much improvement in _____ skills with intensive training.
motor	40. Running, marching, hopping, jumping, climbing, rail walking, using peg boards, pencils, and scissors, sorting objects for size and shape, lifting, and pulling are activities which can be used both to measure and to develop specific motor skills.
	41. Remember that games can provide the retarded child with much more than just a "fun-time." With the correct guidance, playing games can make a valuable contribution to the childs social and physical development. Since the retarded child's intellectual

development will always be limited, social and physical ability may be more important to him than to the normal child.

RECREATION for the retarded

For many retarded persons the experiences of life are limited. The satisfactions and fulfillment that can come through recreation may be of greater importance to them than to the normal person.

Recreation for the retarded becomes even more important when we realize that the majority of retarded persons have much free time and little opportunity to do anything constructive or creative with it.

Recreation for the retarded, in addition to its amusement values, is a training ground for physical skills, social development, and a means of preparation for employment.

Consider, then, that recreation has many goals including the development of *physical capacity, social maturity, leisure time use,* and *employment potential.*

RECREATION FOR RETARDED CHILDREN

	1. All children want and need to play together. Normal children fuse into a group easily, and *group cooperation* comes _____ to them.

naturally, easily	2. Retardates need and want group activities, too, but retardates do not fuse into groups as easily. They must be taught g_____ c_____ .
group cooperation	3. Try to group retardates according to their interests and abilities as well as by their chronological age.
	4. Be careful not to place too much emphasis on mental age in recreation. A child who is eight but has a mental age of three usually should not be grouped with _____ year olds.
three	5. The older child has different social and personal needs to meet as well as a larger _____ to manage.
body	6. Since you cannot expect immediate group _____ , you might try a small group at first.
cooperation	7. After forming a _____ group with similar interests and abilities, you can then plan activities especially for this group.
small	8. Retardates are usually more interested in playing than in following rules and instructions. In choosing activities for them, you would pick games which have _____ rules and require only *simple* instructions.
few	9. Chase, capture, and escape games, such

as "hide and seek," are good basic
_____ for the retarded.

games	10. "Hide and seek" is a good chase, capture, and escape game because it requires few rules and only _____ instructions.

simple	11. It is also a good _____ for retardates because it does not involve *individual competition.*
game	12. Normal children enjoy games involving individual _____ .
competi-tion	13. Retarded children seem to do better in games involving little or no _____ competition.

individual	15. A relay race is a good game activity because it is based on group _____ _____ .
competi- tion	16. It is also a good game because it gives each child a chance to_____ . Enough time should be allowed so that each child can have his turn.
participate, play	17. No child need feel a personal lack of *success* in games involving group _____ .
competi- tion	18. A retarded child's enjoyment of an activity depends a lot upon the amount of _____ he has in doing it.
success	19. Activities should be varied in an effort to bring some _____ to each child.
success	20. Vary the activities. Think of games that are *simple, noncompetitive, instructive,* and still *fun!* You might take games you know normal children like, and _____ them to suit the group.
simplify	21. Be free with praise and encouragement. Praise and _____ are good motivations for retarded children.
encourage- ment	22. All children like to know that you are interested in them and in their activities. Joining in the game shows you are interested.
	23. Retardates will like you to_____

in their games. It is good to take part if you can do so without hindering group participation.

| join, take part | 24. | Aside from the fun, playing games to-gether teaches children to _____ _____ well with each other. |

get along	25.	Cooperation learned in _____ will carry over into other parts of their lives.
games	26.	Always stress the *social* aspects of the game. Remember that one of the goals of recreation is the development of _____ maturity.
social	27.	As they learn fair play and the give-and-take aspect of games, they develop increased social _____ .
maturity	28.	There will be times when a child needs discipline. One good form of _____ is to exclude him from the group.
discipline	29.	Cruel as you may feel it to be, it is better that he be excluded for a short

time than be permanently_____ by the children because he has not learned acceptable behavior.

excluded	30.	Retardates should be encouraged to behave as_____children their age.
normal	31.	For instance, many retardates express their regard for others by being very affectionate.
	32.	You might explain that there are other ways for older boys and girls to express _____ , as with a handshake or a smile.
friendship, affection	33.	Group activities have been stressed and although retardates need and want _____ activities, they also need and want time for *free play*.
group	34.	_____ is a form of *self-expression*.
Free play	35.	Many retardates cannot express their feelings and frustrations verbally or in other acceptable ways, so that free play becomes a form of_____-expression and tension release.
self	36.	Retardates are not as aware of common hazards and dangers as normal children are.
	37.	Because they are not as aware of _____ , they should be closely supervised.

danger	38. The volunteer should not only help _____ the children but should also help them learn rules of safety.
watch, supervise	39. Physical activity is important for retarded children but rest is also important. Retarded children _____ more easily than normal children.
tire	40. Because the children _____ easily and because weather does not always permit outside activities, the volunteer should know what the children need and want to do indoors.
tire	41. Story-telling is one way of providing a period of _____.
rest	42. Retardates frequently do not have as much imagination as normal children. Stories told while looking at _____ or flannel graphs help them to understand the stories better.
pictures	43. Since retardates may lack experience and _____, stories about familiar characters and events are better.
imagina- tion	44. Repetition is important. Many have learned to love the _____ fairy tales and like to help in telling them.
familiar, old	45. The volunteer should always en_____ the children to express themselves.

encourage	46. Retardates cannot pay attention for a long period of time thus they are said to have short _____ spans.
attention	47. Because retardates have short attention spans, in choosing stories for them, it is better to choose _____stories.
short	48. Retardates like "action" stories.

	49. Stories during which the children can stamp their feet, clap their hands, etc., are called _____ stories.
action	50. Action stories allow the children to _____ and this helps to hold their attention.
partici- pate, take part, join in	51. Remember that good stories for retarded children are *short*, contain *familiar* characters and events, and require little imagination. Pictures or flannel graphs should be used generously during the story. The children should be given a chance to *participate* and the stories should be repeated often so that they can help tell the stories themselves.

	52. Music is among the best recreations for retardates. Retarded children love music and respond _____ to it.
naturally, eagerly	53. Simple, repetitive _____ bring immediate enjoyment and response.
songs	54. Just as action stories help hold their attention, so do _____ songs.
action	55. The common kindergarten song, "Where is Thumbkin," is a good _____ song.
action	56. It is an especially good song for retarded children because it helps develop the small _____ in their fingers and hands.
muscles	57. Children like to march, hop, tiptoe, and gallop to music. These activities help to build large _____ and improve coordination.
muscles	58. For those unable to join this type of play, a rhythm band is a good activity.
	59. Rhythm bands also help develop muscles

	and improve _____ .
coordina-tion	60. Making instruments for_____bands can be a simple and useful arts and crafts project.
rhythm	

PRE-TEEN

	61. What about activities for older children? Can they be taught more complicated games such as baseball? Yes___ No___
yes	62. They can, but remember that baseball requires many skills—running, throwing, catching, and batting.
	63. Before actually trying the game of base-ball, these _____ must be developed.
skills	64. Through imitation and repetition, these _____ are slowly learned.
skills	65. Demonstrate each skill thoroughly, then have the children_____ it.
try, repeat	66. Develop each _____ , then build skill upon skill.

skill	67. So that the children do not become bored, try to think of other _____ involving the same skills.
games	68. When they are ready for the actual game of baseball, remember to _____ it to the level of the group.
simplify	69. You might _____ the game by having the children hit the ball, run to one base, and then run home.
simplify, modify	70. Most any activity enjoyed by normal children is suitable for retardates if you _____ it.
simplify	71. Another good activity for those in the pre-teen age group is camping. Camping provides one of the best opportunities for development of the retarded person's physical, social, and creative capacities.

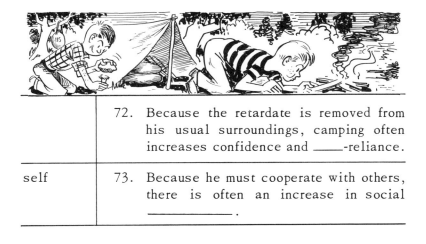

	72. Because the retardate is removed from his usual surroundings, camping often increases confidence and _____-reliance.
self	73. Because he must cooperate with others, there is often an increase in social _____ .

maturity	74. Many retardates are shy and withdrawn. Learning that it is fun to be with others and make friends helps them toward _____ maturity.
social	75. The closeness to nature increases their breadth of interests. Many continuing _____ grow out of camping experiences.
hobbies	76. The ultimate benefit is to bring about closer family unity as the retarded child learns to be more _____.
self-reliant, independent	77. In most camping situations, a volunteer worker is required for each one or two trainable retardates.
	78. Such close supervision is not usually necessary for _____ retardates.
educable	79. The volunteer should always keep in mind the _____ ability and endurance of the campers.
physical	80. A frequent mistake is to push the child too hard. On the other hand, there are times when a little "forceful direction" is needed.
	81. Scouting is another excellent program for the retarded just as it is for _____ children in this age group.
normal	82. Many people think swimming is dangerous

	for the retarded. Swimming is not dangerous but must be closely_____ by people trained in water safety.
watched, super- vised	83. Most cities offer special courses for those who wish to teach swimming to the physically and mentally handicapped.

TEEN-AGE AND ADULT

	84. Do the retarded enjoy social events such as dancing and parties? Yes____ No ____
yes	85. The retarded enjoy and deserve the same type activities as _____ people their age. For teen-age and adult retardates, dancing is a favorite recreation.
normal	86. Dancing is especially good for_____ agers who need and want boy-girl relationships.

teen	87. Dancing provides them with an acceptable way to enjoy boy-girl _____-_____.
relation-ships	88. Square dancing is an excellent activity if it is kept_____.
simple	89. A simple square dance can be made even _____ by using chalk to draw organizational patterns on the floor.
easier, simpler	90. Always give simple, direct instructions. It is better to _____ than to explain.
demon-strate show	91. After _____ slowly and completely, have the group repeat with you what you are doing.
demon-strating	92. In choosing partners, pair a boy who is a good dancer with a girl who is _____ and vice versa.
not	93. Teaching any beginner to dance is discouraging at best, but your enthusiasm and approval will make their learning enjoyable.
	94. Besides dancing, almost any game can be fun for the retarded if you_____ it. Table games, such as ping pong and simplified pool, are excellent activities for the retarded.
simplify	

ARTS AND CRAFTS FOR ALL LEVELS

	95. The goals of recreation are to help the retarded reach his maximum
	  1. _____ capacity,
	  2. _____ maturity,
	  3. use of _____ time, and
	  4. potential for _____ .

physical social leisure employ- ment	96. In achieving these _____ , there is no more important program than arts and crafts.
goals	97. Ideally, it is a program that should start _____ in the retardate's life and continue over a _____ period of time.
early long	98. It is a program through which many of his lifetime habits and attitudes will be shaped.

	99. With your help, he may learn to:
	  1. Work cheerfully because it is fun,
	  2. Work with others, doing his part on a large project,
	  3. Work alone, solving simple problems himself,
	  4. Work steadily toward the satisfaction of completion,
	  5. Listen to and follow directions,
	  6. Take pride in his accomplishments, and
	  7. Work with his hands for his own enjoyment or future employment.

| | 100. | You probably have many original ideas of arts and crafts projects, but let us remind you of a few things you might keep in mind when working with the retarded. |
| | 101. | Retarded persons are not as *creative* as normal people. In choosing a project, be careful that it does not require too much _____. |

creativity	102.	However, you should try to encourage _____ in them when possible.
creativity	103.	In choosing a project, remember to consider first their chronological age, then their _____ age.
mental	104.	Choose simplified versions of projects which normal people their _____ would enjoy.
mental age	105.	Almost all your creative ideas will be useable if you _____ them.

simplify	106. Even a complicated project can be _____ by giving each person one job according to his ability.
simplified	107. For young children, you might choose projects based on seasonal interest. Making a pine cone wreath for Christmas is an example of a _____ project.
seasonal	108. For older retardates, some type of community service project might be included. Making party favors for hospitalized children is a worthwhile _____ project.
service	109. Such projects help the retardate feel he too can contribute something useful to his _____.
community	110. In working with adult retardates, do not forget that they want and deserve _____ activities.
adult	111. Even with adults, however, make sure you keep instructions _____, demonstrating whenever possible.
simple	112. In teaching arts and crafts to any age, keep in mind your goal of developing maximum use of _____ time.
leisure	113. Basic skills should be developed that will enable them to choose _____ of lasting interest and enjoyment.
hobbies	114. Woodworking for boys and sewing for girls are basic _____ that lead to many different hobbies.

skills	115. Besides the use of leisure time, how does the arts and crafts program help the retarded achieve the other goals of recreation?
	116. Working with their hands will help them reach their maximum _____ capacity.
physical	117. Working together will help them reach their maximum _____ maturity.
social	118. The achievement of these two goals and the development of good work habits will help them reach their maximum potential for _____ .
employ- ment	

FAMILY RELATIONS

What about the family of the retarded child?

How does the family relate to the retarded child—and how does the retarded child relate to them?

How may you relate to the family and to the retarded person?

	1. For a family to discover that they have a _____child is a disturbing and upsetting experience.
retarded	2. Understandably, many families are _____ to accept the diagnosis of mental retardation.
slow, reluctant	3. They may spend both time and money seeking a more hopeful diagnosis.
	4. They may cling to the words of friends and even professionals who tell them that their child will _____out of it.
grow	5. They may deny reality by seeking

magical cures or by looking for someone to _____ .

blame	6. The ability of a family group to accept ✓ and adjust to this new experience is determined by a number of factors such as their education, their financial status and their social _____ .

needs, class	7. The "closeness" of a family, the kinds of problems that already exist are other factors that determine the ability of the _____ to cope with this experience.
family	8. A child who will always require that his every _____ be met by others presents a much different problem from one who is educable or trainable.
need	9. A hyperactive or destructive child may

create problems different from those of a child that just sits quietly. In both cases, however, the most important thing is honest acceptance by the family that the problem exists and the realization that only _____ cooperation will solve it.

family	10. The type and severity of the retardation also will have much to do with a family's ability to handle the _____.
situation, problem	11. Parents who will not admit their child is retarded increase their problems and build up even greater _____ tension.
emotional, inner	12. But even parents who admit their child's limitations can't always share their problems because their friends, neighbors and relatives are_____ to ask about the child's welfare.
reluctant, slow	13. Emotional tension is often built up by not being able to satisfactorily_____ their burden with others.
share, talk over	14. They need someone to help them understand their own _____ and attitudes in relation to their handicapped child.
feelings	15. Many retarded people will require guidance and care through their entire _____ span.
life	16. Families often need professional help

in determining how much of their_____
should be spent in relation to the retarded child.

income, money	17. In the early stages the parents need someone who can state in simple terms what mental retardation is and what they can _____ of their retarded child.

expect	18. They need someone who can put them in touch with the community and state agencies that can_____them.
help, aid	19. They need someone to give them guidance in simple basic _____ training.
home, child	20. There is also need for constructive professional comment at various stages in the retarded child's_____.
life	21. Later they will need guidance in deciding upon and providing a _____ program for the child.
training	22. Families must face the problem of what

	will happen to such a child when they are no longer able to care for his _____.
needs	23. Some parents who develop an undue sense of _____ toward the retarded child deny themselves normal family and social activity.
duty	24. Most families love and _____ their retarded child and are able to live comfortably within the community.
accept	25. However, this is not the case in all families, for parents must also cope with problems faced by their _____ children.
normal	26. Especially in the case of a retarded child who looks different, the other children may see him as an embarrassment to them, denying them a _____ social life.
normal	27. They may feel the retarded child requires too much of the parents' _____ or may feel they will be forced into the role of babysitters or caretakers.
time, attention	28. Or to make up for their handicapped brother or sister they may feel pressure to _____ in school.
excel, succeed	29. The retarded child is more _____ than he is different from other children.
like	30. The retarded child first relates to people on an emotional basis. From a strong

	_____ tie, he can be helped to understand himself.
emotional	31. The retarded child responds to the expectations of people he feels are interested in him. If we _____ responsible and acceptable behavior, he will usually give it.
expect	32. The retarded child should never be promised anything unless you expect to follow through. In this way you can help him develop _____ in relationships.
trust	33. The retarded person needs to have the feeling that he is a "person of _____ ."
worth, value	34. The retarded person should have an opportunity to participate in as many _____ as is possible.
activities	35. The retarded child should have nursery group training as soon as possible. This helps him learn to conform to the many social _____ _____ he will face. The nursery group is protective, but at the same time a challenging environment.
demands, expecta- tions	36. The retarded child may need to be taught how to greet people. Volunteers are not Mom, Dad, or Aunt, and the retarded

	child should be taught to _____ them as Mr., Mrs., or Miss.
greet, address	37. The retarded child can be helped to have insight into his limitations if we talk to him in simple language that he can understand. Frequently he does not have insight because we have not given him the background from which to have _____. This applies to behavior of all kinds, including relations with the opposite sex.
insight	38. The retarded child should be _____ to shake hands, not to hug people.
taught	39. The retarded child needs to be taught socially acceptable behavior that is appropriate to his chronological age rather than his _____ age.
mental	40. Help the retarded child to learn _____ behavior with the opposite sex. Often he has never been taught or had the opportunity for such experiences.
appropriate, proper	41. The retarded child needs the same kind of limits (discipline) set for him according to his age and abilities as _____ _____ _____.
any other child, a normal child	42. Help the retarded child to _____ to dress appropriately. Help him to learn the proper fit and help him learn early to dress himself.

learn	43. The retarded child should be started with some task in which he can gain _____. Nothing inspires like success.
success	44. Most important is the fact that the retarded child is usually institutionalized, or loses a job, because of _____ problems (behavior) not because he lacks ability.
social	45. <u>Do/do not</u> become overprotective of the retarded child.
do not	46. Do not let the retarded child become overly _____on you. Help him do things for himself. It may be slower, but it is better for him.

dependent	47. The retarded child should have average tasks broken down into ———— parts.
small	48. The retarded person, if adult, needs to be treated as an adult. Even the retarded person with minimal training and ability can be taught if he knows you are interested in him and that you believe that he can ————.
learn	49. The retarded person needs to be helped to live with some of the ———————— remarks that he is likely to receive from unthinking people.
unkind	50. The retarded person needs to learn that the words "stupid" and "dumb" are a part of our ———————— and may be used without any wrong meaning.
vocabulary, language	51. The retarded person, like all of us, needs to be helped to ———— constructive criticism.

accept	52. The retarded person has the same need for _____ to a family as any other person.
belonging	53. The retarded person should understand that he can want to _____ to his own family even if others do not think his family is right for him.
belong	54. Finally the retarded person needs to become _____ of and to be taught to use community agencies and other community resources.
aware	

BRAIN DAMAGE

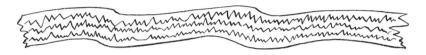

In any discussion of mental retardation, the question of brain damage will eventually be raised. This is one of the most technical and complex areas within the field of retardation. Assessment of brain damage is very difficult. In severe cases, brain damage can be measured by a number of different techniques. In milder brain damage, there is no reliable method of measurement.

The purpose of this section is to present an overview of the relationship between brain damage and retardation and to help the worker become familiar with some of the common forms of brain damage which may be associated with retardation.

	1. Brain damage means injury to the *brain* and the *spinal cord*, or both. The brain and the spinal cord are called the *central nervous system.*
	2. The central nervous system is made up of the _____ and _____ _____.
brain spinal cord	3. D_____ to the central nervous system can take a great number of different forms. It may affect a person's coordination, it may affect any one of his sense

92

	organs, or it may affect his learning ability.
damage	4. What causes brain damage? Brain damage may be caused by any number of child-hood illnesses or injury, including complications during ——————— or birth.
pregnancy	5. Brain damage can cause seeing and hearing defects, not directly of the eyes or ears but of the part of the ——————— that controls seeing and hearing.
brain	6. Brain damage is only one of many ——————— of mental retardation.
causes	7. Only 15 to 25 per cent of all mentally retarded individuals show definite ——————— brain damage which can be specifically identified by neuro-logical tests.
measur-able	8. It is probable that a much larger per-centage of the retarded have some brain damage but not to the extent that can be ———————.
measured	9. Brain damage is not always confined to specific areas of the brain. When brain damage affects several brain areas, several types of ——————— may result.
disability	

EPILEPSY

Many children classified as mentally retarded also have epilepsy. However, not all persons with epilepsy are retarded. Many intellectually normal individuals have epilepsy. "Epilepsy" is the name given to a group of nervous diseases in which the person may have recurrent seizures. A seizure is produced by the uncontrolled release of electrical energy in the brain.

Three common forms of epilepsy are shown in the table on the facing page. Please study this table before starting on the programmed frames, for information from this table will be needed in order to complete some of the frames.

	10. "Epilepsy" is the name given to a group of nervous diseases in which a person may suffer from recurrent _____.
seizures	11. Epilepsy is called a nervous disease because it is due to damage of the _____ _____ _____.
central nervous system	12. There are several types of epilepsy. The most common types are _____ _____ and _____ _____.
grand mal petit mal	13. Loss of consciousness, tightening of muscles, salivation, and possible soiling may indicate a _____ _____ seizure.
grand mal	14. Staring, rhythmic blinking of the eyes, and loss of contact momentarily might indicate a _____ _____ seizure.

TYPES OF EPILEPSY

Type	What happens	Duration	What to do
grand mal epilepsy	Loss of consciousness, tightening of muscles, twitching, tremors, salivation. Possible vomiting or soiling. Coma or deep sleep may follow.	1 or 2 minutes	1. Ease person to floor away from furniture or sharp corners. 2. Loosen clothing. 3. Place on stomach or side. 4. Place folded cloth between teeth if you can do so easily. 5. Provide place for person to sleep. 6. Do not try to stop a seizure.
petit mal epilepsy	Loss of consciousness, eyes may roll up and eyelids may blink rhythmically. Person becomes still and may appear to be staring straight ahead. Lack of awareness.	A few seconds	There is nothing to do except repeat directions that may have been missed while out of contact.
psychomotor epilepsy	Automatic movements such as rubbing hands across chest in purposeless fashion. Person may act violently, then not remember what he has done. May appear to be having temper tantrum. (Not as common a form of epilepsy as grand mal and petit mal)	Varying but brief periods	In case of any type seizure, a person in authority should be notified. Remain calm so that you do not alarm others.

petit mal	15. "Bad" behavior or a brief period of automatic, pointless behavior may indicate _____ epilepsy.
psycho-motor	16. You should _always/never_ attempt to stop a seizure.
never	17. The first thing to do is to see that the person does not _____ himself on furniture or sharp corners.
injure	18. A person can't "swallow" his tongue but a small rolled up wad of handkerchief or some such material can keep him from biting it. Never place a _____ object in his mouth.

metal, solid	19. After a grand mal seizure there may be unconsciousness or a state of confusion for a short time. It is best to have a person remain _____ until you feel sure he is back in control of himself.
resting, inactive	20. Epilepsy today is not nearly as frightening a problem as it was years ago. Medical advances have made it possible to _____ most cases of epilepsy.

control	21. The volunteer should always _____ a seizure to a person in authority, since a change in medication may be necessary.
report	22. One of the most important things that a volunteer can do is to learn not to fear epilepsy. It may be best to look upon a seizure as a form of unconsciousness or fainting. It may help to realize that a person is not suffering when he has a seizure, he is merely expressing uncontrollable central nervous system activity.

CEREBRAL PALSY

Many people confuse cerebral palsy and mental retardation. Many individuals classified as retarded also may have cerebral palsy. Cerebral palsy is a nerve and muscle disorder which results from damage to the central nervous system. People at all levels of intelligence may have cerebral palsy. It is important to realize that mental retardation and cerebral palsy may exist independently of each other. This distinction is stressed because a person with cerebral palsy may appear to be retarded because of his lack of muscular control or poor communication even though he may have superior intelligence.

Cerebral palsy takes many different forms and varies according to the location and extent of the damage to the central nervous system. There are several different types of cerebral palsy, but they are all so much alike it is not important for the volunteer to be able to identify the different types.

The most common types are spastic, athetoid, and ataxic. All forms of cerebral palsy involve a lack of control of muscle movements. The muscles often remain tense and movements may be jerky. Persons affected may walk in a lurching, stumbling manner and may have poor control over their facial expressions.

Although the term "cerebral palsy" refers to muscular control, many individuals have additional handicaps due to brain damage such as mental retardation, seizures, vision, hearing, or speech defects. Approximately 50 per cent of the cerebral palsied may be classified as mentally retarded.

	23. Cerebral palsy is a term used to describe a number of types of muscular disabilities resulting from _____ _____.
brain damage	24. A person with cerebral palsy is unable to control the movements of his _____ because that part of his brain that tells the muscles what to do has been _____.
muscles damaged	25. The disability of cerebral palsy varies from mild motor incoordination to complete helplessness. The amount of disability differs according to the _____ and amount of brain damage.
location, area	26. A person afflicted with cerebral palsy often/seldom has additional handicaps.
often	27. Among the cerebral palsied, approximately _____ per cent are classified as retarded.
50	

THE HYPERACTIVE CHILD

Some brain-damaged children show no obvious physical defect but may have disturbances of learning and behavior. Such a child is often described as hyperactive.

	28.	Although such children may show no _____ defects, they do show disturbance of learning and general behavior because of _____ _____ .
physical brain damage	29.	The child's behavior is called _____ _____ .
hyper- active, overactive	30.	The hyperactive child will always be on the go. He will find sitting still very _____ .
difficult, trying	31.	Very often it is difficult for a volunteer to accept hyperactivity. She may feel the child just does not want to _____ .

behave	32. If she will observe carefully, however, she will be able to see a difference between the children who are able to respond to structure or discipline and _____ children.
hyperactive	33. There is a very important difference between these two types of children.
	34. A hyperactive child does not mean to be difficult, he just cannot _____ his behavior.
control, help, regulate	35. A hyperactive child may have a very _____ attention span. When he starts something he probably won't finish it. It is difficult for him to stick to anything.
short	36. One of the most difficult things for a volunteer to understand may be the child's radical changes in behavior. One day he may do a job very well, the next day he may do just the _____.
opposite	37. You can't _____ how the child is going to react from one situation to another.
predict	38. Just as the child is overactive physically, he is also overactive _____. He will be inclined towards extremes of laughter and crying.
emotion-ally	39. Since the hyperactive child has such poor control over his feelings and

	actions, a great deal of extra _____ is required on the teacher's part.
attention	40. The teacher may have to continue to _____ the child for his attention to the task assigned him.
reward, praise	41. The hyperactive child is easily distracted, so it is best to keep his surroundings as _____ as possible.
simple	42. Give him something to do that has definite _____ to it. Attempt to help him make order out of his confusing existence
structure, limits	

You may be able to recognize a hyperactive child by some of the following behavior characteristics:
1. He is always on the go,
2. He has poor concentration,

3. He is unpredictable,
4. He is impulsive,
5. He has poor emotional control,
6. He tends to have poor coordination, and
7. He has considerable difficulty with reading, writing, and in choosing words to express himself.

The hyperactive child may be helped by special medication and by psychotherapy. In addition, special teaching methods have been developed to help him learn and adjust.

The volunteer worker can help by being able to recognize a hyperactive child and appreciate the fact that his behavior, no matter how inappropriate is not fully under his control. She can aid by helping to direct his behavior and by relieving the constant pressure that his behavior places on teachers or other persons in charge.

SPEECH AND HEARING

Have you ever been lost in a sea of words? Almost everyone has at some time or other—perhaps during a technical lecture you shouldn't have attended in the first place, perhaps listening to a nuclear scientist on television or even to an instructor when you have fallen behind the class.

If you have ever suffered such an experience, then you have some idea of how it must feel to the mentally retarded child who has not yet learned to use our most valued tool of communication—words—and thus lives in a world of sounds he does not understand.

1. Since the mentally retarded child is slow in learning even the simplest skills, we should not be surprised to find him _____ in learning such a complicated skill as speech.

103

slow	2. A common problem among the mentally retarded is "delayed speech." When a child reaches the age of three and is still unable to speak in a way that others can understand, he may be said to have _____ speech.
delayed	3. Speech is a useful tool by which you _____ with others, control others, and express your feelings. A child without this tool is severely handicapped.
communi-cate	4. A lisper, stutterer, or laller is not so handicapped for he only needs help in perfecting _____ that is already useful to him.
speech	5. But the child with _____ speech must first be helped to build his speech skills and then be taught how to use them effectively.
delayed	6. How do you start in helping him to build his speech skills?

	7. The best way to start is by helping him learn to listen, or pay _____ to certain sounds or words.

attention	8. Many retarded children seem not to pay attention to _____ .
sounds	9. Yet careful _____ to sounds is necessary for speech learning.
attention	10. However, another reason for not paying attention is the lack of _____ many sounds or words have for a retarded child.
meaning	11. The physical ability to hear is not enough unless the child associates a certain sound with its proper _____ .
meaning	12. Usually the first meaningful sound to a child is his mother's voice which he learns to _____ with comfort, warmth, food, and love.
associate	13. Through hearing a word over and over, in a way that is meaningful to him, he learns to _____ sound and meaning.
associate	14. When a child is able to associate word sounds with their proper _____ , he takes his first step toward speech.
meanings	15. Children talk because they want to, not because parents _____ them to.
want	16. Some parents try to _____ a child to speak before he is ready.
force	17. There is a special time when each child is _____ for word learning.

ready	18. When a child is _____ to learn words, then words are taught more easily and learned more readily.
ready	19. Before this special _____, it is almost impossible to teach speech. If the special time is passed, teaching becomes increasingly difficult.
time, period	20. Simple words are said to a baby, and when he is able to understand their _____, he begins to use them himself.
meaning	21. A normal child will begin to use_____ words at about one year (10 to 18 months).
simple	22. A _____ child may not be ready either to understand or use words until between eighteen months and four years of age.
retarded	23. By then he is running around and people are talking to him in complete _____ _____.
sentences	24. He can't understand complete sentences until he can understand _____ words.
simple	25. He could now be learning the _____ words but they are no longer being presented to him.
simple	26. He may ignore what people say because he doesn't _____ what is being said.

under-stand	27. The longer he goes without help the more he may develop the habit of _____what people say.
ignoring	28. Since he has so few people he can talk to he becomes his own mirror and model of poor and limited _____.
speech	29. He gets very little satisfaction from communication since he cannot make his wants _____.
known	30. As he is hard to understand, those around him may hinder his speech learning further by anticipating his _____.
wants	31. Words are tools, and if not needed, they will not be _____.
used	32. Retarded children are also hindered in speech development by impatient adults who begin to _____ speech rather than *reward* it.
demand, require	33. Children need to learn that _____, such as adult attention and getting what they want, can come when they talk.

rewards	34. These _____ will often give the child the motivation he needs for learning to talk.
rewards	

HOW THE VOLUNTEER CAN HELP

Many of you will not work directly with children in a speech clinic. However, as a volunteer, you have an important role to play in the development of speech of the retarded while you are with them in the classroom, on the playground, or elsewhere.

Following are some practical ways you can help the mentally retarded toward better speech.

	35. First, let's look at the child who does not talk or who is very hesitant to talk.
	36. Asking him to say a specific word, even though it may result in occasional success, in the long run creates _____ delay.
speech	37. He begins to think of talking as something which he can't do very well. He gets tense about it, and _____ becomes more feared than rewarding to him.
it, talking	38. Before trying to get him to talk, try to get to know each other through sharing activities. This will help build his _____ in you.
trust,	39. Then you might encourage him to say

confidence	one word, gradually increasing the number of words to form simple _____.
phrases, sentences	40. This can be done by what is called *parallel talking*.
	41. Parallel _____ is done by putting yourself in the child's place and saying the necessary word or phrase at the very instant the child should be needing it.
talking	42. If the child appears to be predicting that Jack will jump out of his box, you might say, "Jack pop out." If he pricks his finger, you might say _____.

"Ow! Ow! Hurt!"	43. This may sound like baby talk to you, but it isn't. It is part of putting his immediate _____ into words.
feelings, thoughts	44. Remember to _____ all hard or un- necessary words, much as you would for a person who is learning a foreign language.

avoid, remove	45. The next step may be to show the child that words are magical tools that will get him what he _____ .
wants, desires	46. This can be done by commanding dolls, puppets, or even ourselves to fall down, cry, and clap hands, making them _____ .
obey, do it	47. As the child watches, he sees the power of _____ , and soon he is commanding too.
words, speech	48. "Tool" words, rather than "display" words, should be _____ .
empha- sized, used	49. "Throw ball," "go out," "mine," are examples of _____ words.

tool	50. Teaching a child to repeat phrases, such as "Hello, how are you?", al- though nice, does not show him how words can get him what he wants. These are merely _____ words.
display	51. Many children use gestures rather than _____ ..

words	52. Provide the simple words they need, repeat them often, and when the child begins to use them, reinforce them with _____ .
rewards, praise, encourage- ment	53. When a child pulls you toward the door and gestures to go outside, hesitate just a moment as though you don't under- stand, then say, "Oh, outside, go out- side." Then *go*.

WORKING ON SPEECH SOUNDS

	54. Again, remember that *direct correction* in the language learning stage may shut the child's speech valve off. Direct _____ discourages language learning.
correction	55. By direct correction we mean saying to the child: "Don't say 'thoup,' say 'sssoup.' Now, say 'sssoup,' etc."
	56. Interrupting a child, especially to _____ him, can do a great deal of harm.
correct	57. It is important to wait calmly, _____ with interest, until the child has said what he has to say.
listening	58. Constant fear of interruption is among the many factors that contribute to _____ .
stuttering	59. Practice on speech _____ should

	wait until the child has a sizable vocabulary and uses some phrases.
sounds	60. Speech sounds can be taught by stressing the sounds the child needs in words *after* he has said them rather than correcting him directly or_____ him.
interrupting	61. For example when the child says "tor" the volunteer says simply, "fffffor."
	62. Work on only one sound at a time.

Here is an example of how you might go about helping a child who is hesitant to talk: Let's assume he already has gotten to like and trust you. Before meeting with him, think of the words you wish to teach and a likely situation for teaching them. During the first part of the meeting, repeat the words over and over as you play with an appropriate toy. Then set the same situation up again only with things arranged so that the child is in the role you were in. For instance, you may say, "Here goes the truck, here goes the truck, here goes the truck, ooops, fell off the table!" Then give the child the truck, saying the same thing but omitting a word for him to fill in. He might start with "oooooop," but that, at least, is a start.

Always reward, through smiles, warmth, and praise, the child's best efforts to talk.

There are a number of health specialists in your community who work together in the care of the mentally retarded. One of these specialists is the Public Health Nurse.

The primary function of the Public Health Nurse is teaching the prevention of disease and the promotion of health, not only through public schools and clinics but through direct contact with families in their homes.

Teaching the need for early medical care and seeing that it is received during pregnancy is one way in which she helps prevent mental retardation. Another is through early recognition of diseases such as meningitis which may cause retardation if not given prompt medical care.

Early recognition, evaluation, and follow-up can also lead to the proper handling of a retarded child to prevent emotional problems and help him reach his maximum potential for development.

	1. Being a keen observer in all of her contacts with a child is one of the Public Health Nurse's most valuable services.
	2. The nurse will expect you as a volunteer to also be a keen _____.
observer	3. Here are some of the things she will expect you to observe and in some

instances record. (Some, of course, you will want to report immediately to the person in charge.) As a volunteer, you should always:

4. Watch for sores, bruises, rashes, and swollen or reddened areas. Some of these may be indications of contagious diseases and should be _____ immediately.

reported	5. Note the child's eyes. Bright, clear eyes are usually a sign of health. Glassy, tearful, dull, or red eyes are signs of possible fever or _____.
sickness	6. Observe how the child holds his body and what he does with his arms and legs. He may be unable to _____ you he has pain and you will only know by watching him. For instance, tugging on an ear may indicate a painful or infected ear.

tell	7. Observe for staring spells and periods when the child seems out of _____ with you. These may be indications of seizures and may need to be investigated further.
contact, touch	8. Watch to see if he is constantly on the move or if he just seems to sit all the time. The retarded child may do either, and often medicine can change his behavior, letting him take part in group _____ and thus helping him progress.
activities	9. Some retarded children take medicine daily. Observe the child's ability to get about. Is he steady on his feet? Does he stagger? Can he run, hop? His inability or unsteadiness may indicate that the _____ he takes needs to be changed.
medicine	10. Observe how he behaves toward you and others. Does he cry or smile at the right time? Does he take up for himself? Does he strike out at others? Notice changes in his behavior, for they can indicate the beginnings of _____ problems.
emotional	11. Observe his ability to chew and swallow at mealtime. His food may need to be chopped or pureed. He may need small _____ more often so that he may take in enough food.

meals	12. Regular handling and routine are necessary for the retarded child. This means that there must be good understanding among those who work with the child. This is one reason why _____ and reporting are an important part of the volunteer's work.
observing	

THE EFFECT OF A RETARDED CHILD ON THE FAMILY

Having a retarded child places many additional stresses on the family. Of course, the threat to the family varies tremendously according to the severity of the child's handicap, the family's ability to deal with problem situations, and their income.

As a volunteer in some settings, you may have contact with the families of retarded persons and should be aware of the problems they face. Perhaps by hearing what some family members have to say, you will understand better some of the problems they face. Listen to a mother:

> The children are crazy about Lucy, but they rarely bring their friends home. It's not that they're ashamed or anything, it's just that we seldom have a quiet evening. She's into everything and needs attention every minute. One evening every member of the family had an engagement. I phoned to a neighbor and asked her to look after Lucy for just an hour. My oldest son heard me and said, "I'll stay home and take care of her." He wouldn't go to his practice. I don't want the other children to give up everything.

Or a father:

> We don't live like other married people. We don't go out together any more. When we finally find a baby sitter who's willing to take care of Matt, we find we can't trust her with him. We fight a lot but I don't think it's the babys fault—I think it's because we never go out and have fun together.

Or a sister:

> Since my sister was born I feel like I hardly have a mother anymore. She spends all her time and energy on her. I know it's hard and she can't help the way things are but she's so tired by night she can't even talk to me. Sometimes I have problems but mostly I'd just like to tell her about stuff that happens at school and things like that.

These are not complaints—they are situations that are very real to families who have mentally retarded children. The love they feel for the retarded child is great, but the stress on the family is equally great. Many of these families need more help and help over a longer period of time than those with other kinds of problems.

Many of the problems are eased as the retarded child learns to care for himself. Seeing that the child learns to care for himself is an important task of the Public Health Nurse. She does this through helping the family look for signs of readiness to learn and through discussing and demonstrating the best ways of teaching the child. Here are some of the things she tells parents about self-care which should also prove valuable to you as a volunteer.

13. Begin with what the child is ready to learn. He will show interest in what he is _____ to learn. You may have to look hard for signs of his being ready

	since he may not show it as clearly as a normal child. Never use his age as a guide.
ready	14. The more *severe* the handicap, the more *slowly* you will have to teach, the more you will have to *repeat,* and the more important it is that you _____ the same way each time.
repeat	15. Use few words—tell him and _____ him at the same time.
show	16. Teach only _____ step at a time.
one	17. Even though it be with just a smile, see that each small success is
rewarded, praised	18. Teach each activity at a natural time for doing it so that it has meaning, such as dressing when he gets up in the morning and self-feeding at _____ .
mealtime	19. Be sure that you have the child's attention when you are showing and telling. Call his name, touch him, and direct his face and _____ to what you are doing.
attention	20. He is not only slow to learn, but it is hard for him to get rid of bad habits. He is apt to learn what he sees, so be sure that the behavior he sees is _____ behavior for him to copy.
good	21. He is very sensitive to your tone of voice. He may not always understand

what you say, but he will usually recognize your feelings from your tone. Your actions and _____ _____ _____ should show a warm, pleasant attitude.

tone of voice	

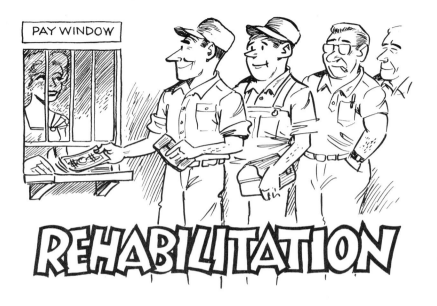

REHABILITATION

Today and each day of the year 350 new parents will hear for the first time the words, "Your child is retarded."

If you were one of these parents, what would be your reaction? What steps would you take? If your child was retarded, how would it affect his life? And how would it affect your life?

For these parents of a retarded child, "rehabilitation" takes on a very real meaning.

The purpose of this section is to help you obtain a basic understanding of the rehabilitation process as it affects the life of a retarded child and his family.

1. The word "rehabilitation" is a new word in our vocabulary. Twenty years ago very few people used the word. Today most people have heard it. But

	just what does the word _____ actually mean?
rehabilita-tion	2. The word "rehabilitation" means the "restoration" of a person to as much independence and productivity as possible. The _____ process assists a handicapped person to make the most of his potential as an active member of society.
rehabilita-tion	3. Many people think that the rehabilitation of handicapped persons is limited to medical services. In many cases, medical services. may begin the process but they are not usually the_____ answer.
whole, total	4. The central theme of rehabilitation is to work with the_____person. This involves helping a handicapped person in all phases of life which may be necessary for him to achieve as much independence and productivity as possible.

whole	5. Achieving independence and _____-_____ may involve help in many areas of life. A handicapped person may need help with emotional problems, special training to learn a new skill, assistance in finding a job, and other special services.
produc- tivity	6. The rehabilitation process can become quite complex when several problems are involved. Many different services and years of time may be required in rehabilitating a severely handicapped person.
	7. In recent years more and more attention has been placed upon the _____ of the mentally retarded.
rehabilita- tion	8. The rehabilitation of retarded children may be quite different from the problems involved in restoring a physically handicapped adult to _____ and productivity.
indepen- dence	9. The retarded child usually is handicapped from very early in life and basic skills must be *developed* rather than *restored*.
	10. For this reason the word "habilitation" is usually used instead of "rehabilitation" when talking about a handicap that has existed from birth.
	11. _____ refers to the development

	of basic skills which enable a person to take a productive place in society.
habilita-tion	12. The first step in habilitation of retarded individuals is *identification of the problem*.
	13. In the case of the trainable or severely retarded child the condition is usually apparent at _____ or in the first few years of life.
birth	14. In such cases the habilitation process is of necessity, started at a very early age in the home because the child may need special help in learning basic self-care skills such as dressing, toilet training, and feeding himself.

	15. The earlier the _____ process can start, the better.

habilita- tion	16. Preschool or nursery school programs are very helpful to _____ children, if available in the community.
trainable	17. In many cases the trainable child is not able to enter regular school classes and usually either private or public special schools are sought by the parents to help the child.
	18. The goal of habilitation with the trainable child is usually limited to the development of basic life skills to help the child achieve as much independence and _____ as possible.
self-care	19. Because the trainable child is frequently physically handicapped, medical services may play a central role in _____. In addition, many specialized services such as speech therapy and special school training may be utilized.
habilita- tion	20. The trainable child seldomly enters into competitive industry, so vocational training is usually limited to living semi-independently at home or working under supervision in a sheltered workshop.

THE EDUCABLE RETARDED CHILD

	21. With the educable mentally retarded, identification of the problem is frequently

	much more difficult and complex than with the _____ retarded child.
trainable	22. Many times the problem of _____ is not recognized until the child is in the first few years of public school.
retarda-tion	23. In talking about the educable child, we must remember that there is a wide range of differences among educable children.
	24. Many educable retarded children will have difficulty in the first or second grade of school. However, in some cases an _____ child may be able to "pass" several grades of school before a serious problem becomes apparent.
educable	25. As the child runs into increasing difficulty in school work and drops behind his classmates, the school and parent will usually call in professional help to understand the child's problem.
	26. A series of specialized tests is usually used to arrive at a diagnosis of the problem.

	27. The diagnosis of retardation is usually based upon a psychological evaluation administered by a professional psychologist. Although the score of an I.Q. test is often used, it should be noted that a number of factors are taken into account in establishing a _____ of retardation.
diagnosis	28. Many times, _____ of mental retardation is more complex than has been outlined above. Speech and/or hearing problems may be involved, medical problems are not uncommon and the child may also have emotional problems.
diagnosis, identification	29. When identification of retardation has established as at least part of the child's problem, the next stage of the _____ process is *planning*.
habilitation	30. Planning may include recognizing the need for specialized medical services, placing the child in special education classes and obtaining professional help for children with emotional problems.
	31. In the past decade a great many school systems have started "sp_____ education classes" to offer a learning situation which will be scaled to the slower development of the retarded child.
special	32. From this point it is difficult to make general statements as to what course habilitation may take because services

	must be determined by the individual case to be most effective.
	33. Placing emphasis on individual habilitation programs is very well recognized and followed by professional workers in the field.

VOCATIONAL REHABILITATION

	34. As stated in the beginning of this section, the goal of the rehabilitation process is to help handicapped persons achieve the highest degrees of _____ which they are capable.
independence	35. In the case of _____ retarded children, independence may mean the development of self-care skills.
trainable	36. These _____ skills may range from learning to feed themselves to such things as learning how to ride a bus.
self-care	37. More than 75 per cent of all retarded individuals fall into the higher level— the educable group. The goal of habilitation with _____ retarded individuals is to help them find employment as they reach early adulthood.
educable	38. Many retarded children require considerable special training to enable them to be capable of even unskilled labor. The problems of the retarded child may be quite different from the

	nonretarded when it comes to _____ or _____ training.
job voca- tional	39. It is common to think of the world of work merely in terms of technical skills. This is a big mistake. There are many basic social skills which are far more important than _____ skills on any job.

technical	40. We usually take these basic _____ skills for granted because most of us develop these skills somewhat naturally through experience—but this is not the case with most retarded young adults.
social	41. Training programs to prepare the re- tarded for the work world would usually be called pre _____ or ''per- sonal adjustment'' training.
vocational	42. What social skills are we speaking of? Such things as dependability, going to work every day, and being on time. Ability to use public transportation in getting to _____ is an important social skill which a retarded person may lack.

work	43. The ability to stay in one place for a number of hours, the ability to keep attention on the task, learning to take _____ from a supervisor, and learning to get along with other employees are just a few of the many social skills which are necessary to hold a job in competitive industry.
orders, directions	44. Without these basic social skills, the most skilled _____ could not hold a job.
technician	45. It may take as long as two or three years of prevocational training after leaving school for some retarded children to _____ these skills.
learn, acquire	46. _____ vocational training programs can take many different forms. They are most commonly found in: (1) public school programs for the retarded, (2) sheltered workshops for the handicapped, and (3) state institutions for the retarded. For clarification we will deal with each of these separately, although there is frequently a close association between schools, sheltered workshops, and state institutions.
Pre	

PUBLIC SCHOOL PROGRAMS

	47. Special education classes in the public schools are continually placing more emphasis upon training the educable mentally retarded in basic _____ skills needed in the work would rather than just stressing the ''3 R's.''
social	48. These _____ _____ classes frequently train older children in use of want-ads, use of public transportation, making change, etc.
special education	49. In addition, a number of school systems have started ''work-experience programs'' for the retarded. Educable mentally retarded adolescents cannot usually meet the academic requirements of a technical trade school.

	50. In some work- _____ programs the retardates will actually work on a job in the community as a part of every school day.

experience	51. Other work-experience programs provide the child with training by having him work in the school cafeteria or some other department within the_____.
school	

SHELTERED WORKSHOPS

	52. A sheltered workshop is an industrial or craft shop which is set up to employ handicapped individuals who _____ meet the requirement of competitive industry.
cannot	53. In the past ten years more than 400 _____ workshops have been established in the country.
sheltered	54. Some sheltered workshops are relatively large industries employing hundreds of _____ workers, but most are small shops which employ less than twenty-five persons.

handi- capped	55. Some sheltered workshops are connected with a public school system, some are operated by community agencies, and some are privately supported. Almost all sheltered workshops require some type of community support; very few, if any, are self-supporting from the sale of products alone.
	56. In communities where sheltered workshops exist it is becoming quite common for a retarded child to enter the sheltered workshop as soon as he _____ public school classes usually at age 16 or 18).
leaves	57. The retarded child may attend a sheltered workshop for only a few months and be able to find outside employment at that time—or, in some cases he may _____ be able to enter outside employment and may stay at the sheltered workshop for several years.
never	58. In the protective atmosphere of a sheltered workshop the demands on production are limited to the capability of the handicapped person.
	59. For many years, state institutions for the retarded have had older patients working in different departments of the institution as kitchen help, yard workers, laundry workers, etc. In many cases the purpose of this work was mainly just to keep the patients _____ .

busy	60. During the past ten or twenty years, most state institutions have set up active training programs to help prepare clients to _____ their home communities.
return	61. Many of the institutional training programs find job training situations for the clients near the _____ .
institu-tion	62. In these cases the retarded individual will live in the institution at night, and go out each day to _____ in the community.
work	63. Most institutions have set up "half-way" houses for these individuals. A _____ _____ house is a special cottage where the patients live much more independently than they would in the regular institution cottages or wards.
halfway	

SELECTED BIBLIOGRAPHY

Rehabilitation

Fraenkel, William A.: *The Mentally Retarded and Their Vocational Rehabilitation: A Resource Handbook*. National Association for Retarded Children, 1961.

Pinkard, Calvin M., Jr.: Alden S. Gilmore, Lawrence H. Ricker, and Charles F. Williams: *Predicting Vocational Capacity of Retarded Young Adults*. Tampa, MacDonald Training Center Foundation, 1963.

Rogers, D. P.: Development of a Statewide Program for the Vocational Rehabilitation of the Mentally Retarded: A Report on an OVR Demonstration Grant—Project N., RD537, Charleston, West Virginia, 1962.

Southern Methodist University: Rehabilitation and Research in Retardation: Proceedings of a Conference on the Vocational Rehabilitation of the Mentally Retarded held at Dallas, Texas, February 10-12, 1960. National Association for Retarded Children.

U. S. Department of Health, Education and Welfare: *Preparation of Mentally Retarded Youth for Gainful Employment*. Washington, U. S. Government Printing Office, 1959.

U. S. Department of Health, Education and Welfare: Proceedings of a Conference on Special Problems in Vocational Rehabilitation of the Mentally Retarded held in Madison, Wisconsin, November 3-7, 1963.

University of Kansas: *A Report on the Institute of Sheltered Workshop Services for the Mentally Retarded*. Goodwill Industries of America, 1961.

Medical

American Medical Association: *Mental Retardation: A Handbook for the Preliminary Physician*. A report on the American Medical Association conference on Mental Retardation, April 9-11, 1964.

Guthrie, Robert, and Steward Whitnew: *Phenylketonuria Detection in the Newborn as a Routine Hospital Procedure*. Washington, U. S. Government Printing Office, 1964.

U. S. Department of Health, Education and Welfare: *The Care of the Retarded Child: Therapy and Prognosis*. Washington, U. S. Government Printing Office, 1964.

Volunteers

Adult Education Association of the USA: *Working With Volunteers*. Chicago, 1960.

134

Ball, Edith L.: *Developing Volunteers for Service in Recreation Programs*. New York, National Recreation Association, 1958.

Connecticut Department of Mental Health: *Volunteer Service Development in State Programs for the Mentally Ill and Retarded*. Proceedings of a Conference for Hospital Administrators and Directors of Volunteer Programs held in Stratford, Connecticut, November 11-16, 1960. National Institutes of Health, Bethesda, Maryland.

Rich, Thomas A., and Alden S. Gilmore: Volunteer work with the retarded. *Ment. Retard.*, August, 1964.

Rich, Thomas A., Alden S. Gilmore, and Charles F. Williams: Volunteer work with the mentally retarded. *Rehab. Rec.*, September-October, 1964.

Recreation

American Camping Association: *Directory of Camps for the Handicapped*. Martinsville, Indiana, American Camping Association, 1966.

Benoit, E. Paul: *The Psycho-Educational Implications of Play in Retarded Children*. New York, National Association for Retarded Children, Inc.

Benoit, E. Paul: The Play Problem of Retarded Children. *Amer. J. Ment. Defic.*, July, 1955.

Boy Scouts of America. *Scouting with Mentally Retarded Boys*. New Brunswick, N. J., Boy Scouts of America.

Caldwell, Stratton: Aqatics for the mentally retarded. *Swimming Pool Age*, June, 1957.

Delph, Harold A.: How can we help him? *Scouting*, July-August, 1954.

Francis, Robert J., and Rasick G. Lawrence: *Motor Characteristics of the Mentally Retarded*. Washington, U. S. Government Printing Office, 1960.

Girl Scouts of America: *Girl Scouting for the Handicapped*. New York, Girl Scouts of America.

Larson, Roland: The mentally retarded at camp; community teamwork is vital. *Recreation*, March, 1957.

National Association for Retarded Children: *Directory of Day Camps Serving the Mentally Retarded*. New York. 1964.

National Association for Retarded Children: *Directory of Residential Camps Serving the Mentally Retarded*. New York, 1964.

National Association for Retarded Children: *Retarded Children Can Go Camping*. New York.

National Health and Welfare Association: Developing skills for the retarded child. *Recreation*, December, 1954.

Ontario Recreation Association: *A Pilot Study of Swimming for the Severely Mentally Retarded*. Oshawa, Ontario, Committee on Recreation for the Retarded.

Ontario Recreation Association: *A Playground for Severely Mentally Retarded Children*. Oshawa, Ontario, Committee on Recreation for the Retarded.

Schlotter, B., and M. Svendsen: *An Experiment in Recreation with the Mentally Retarded*. Chicago, Illinois Department of Welfare.

Sember, Andrew T.: A critique of summer recreational and craft activities for mentally retarded children. *Train. Sch. Bull. (Vineland)*, November, 1957.

Smith, J. E.: Camping with the mentally retarded. *Recreation*, September, 1953.

Southern Regional Education Board Recreation Committee: *Recreation for the Mentally Retarded*. Atlanta, SREB Attendant Training Project, 1964.

Rich, Thomas A., and Alden S. Gilmore: *You're It: A Training Film for Recreation Leaders Working With the Mentally Retarded*. MacDonald Training Center Foundation, 1966.

Religion

Lerrigo, Marion O.: *The Mentally Retarded and the Church*. New York, National Association of Churches of Christ in the USA.

National Association for Retarded Children, Inc.: A selected bibliography on Religion and Religious Education, New York, 1963.

Bibliographies

American Association on Mental Deficiency. *Mental Retardation Abstracts*. National Clearinghouse for Mental Health Information, National Institute of Mental Health, Bethesda, Maryland.

Freeburg, William H., and Garold W. Eaglin: *Recreation for the Handicapped: A Bibliography*. Information Center—Recreation for the Handicapped, Southern Illinois University, 1965.

National Association for Retarded Children: *A Basic Library on Mental Retardation*. New York, 1963.

National Association for Retarded Children: *A Selected Bibliography on Religion and Religious Education*. New York: 1963.

National Institute of Child Health and Human Development, Public Health Service: Supplement to Bibliography of World Literature on Mental *Retardation: March, 1963—December, 1964*. Public Health Service No. 1316.

Governmental

President's Panel on Mental Retardation: *Report of the Task Force on Prevention, Clinical Services and Residential Care*. Washington, U. S. Department of Health, Education, and Welfare, Public Health Service, 1962.

President's Panel on Mental Retardation: *Mental Retardation: A National Plan for a National Problem*. Washington, U. S. Government Printing Office, 1963.

U. S. Department of Health, Education and Welfare: *Mental Retardation: Activities of the U. S. Department of Health, Education, and Welfare*.

U. S. Department of Health, Education, and Welfare: *The White House Conference on Mental Retardation: Proceedings*. Washington, U. S. Government Printing Office, 1963.

Education and Training

Baumgartner, Bernice B.: *Helping the Trainable Mentally Retarded Child*. New York, Bureau of Publications, Teachers College, Columbia University, 1960.

Cleverdon, Dorothy: A Work-Play Program for the Trainable Mental Deficient. *Amer. J. Ment. Defic.*, July, 1955.

Ebling, George, Jr.: Some aspects of a community program for educable mentally retarded children. *Amer. J. Ment. Defic.*, April, 1954.

Hart, Evelyn: *How Retarded Children Can Be Helped*. New York, Public Affairs Committee, Inc., 1962.

Jacob, Walter: *New Hope for the Retarded Child*. New York, Public Affairs Committee, 1954.

Kelman, J. R.: A program for mentally retarded children. *Children*, January–February, 1955.

McBride, Ruth: Community planning to meet some of the social needs of the mentally retarded adult. *Amer. J. Ment. Defic.*, July, 1953.

McDermott, William H.: Art therapy for the severely handicapped. *Amer. J. Ment. Defic.*, October, 1954.

Malpass, Leslie F., Alden S. Gilmore, Miles W. Hardy, and Charles F. Williams: *Comparison of Two Automated Teaching Procedures for Retarded Children*. Tampa, University of South Florida, 1963.

Malpass, Leslie F., Alden S. Gilmore, Miles W. Hardy, and Charles F. Williams: *Automated Teaching for Retarded Children: A Summary Comparison of Two Procedures*. U. S. Department of Health, Education, and Welfare, Office of Education, Cooperative Research Program, 1963.

Malpass, Leslie F., Alden S. Gilmore, Miles W. Hardy, and Charles F. Williams: Programmed instruction for retarded children. *Programmed Teaching*, Joseph S. Roucek, Ed. New York, Philosophical Library.

Schorsch, J. J.: Music therapy for the physically or mentally handicapped child. *Education*, March, 1950.

Parents

Cianci, Vencentz: Home training for the mentally retarded child.

Children, May—June, 1955.

Dittmann, Laura L.: *The Mentally Retarded Child at Home: A Manual for Parents.* Washington, U. S. Government Printing Office.

Kramm, Elizabeth R.: *Families of Mongoloid Children.* Washington, U. S. Government Printing Office, 1963.

Morrison, Marcia: *Now They Are Gorwn!* New York, National Association for Retarded Children, 1960.

U. S. Department of Health, Education, and Welfare: *The Mongoloid Baby.* U. S. Government Printing Office, 1962.

Weingold, Joseph T.: Parent's groups and the problem of mental retardation. *Amer. J. Ment. Defic.,* January, 1952.

Williams, Harold M.: *The Retarded Child Goes to School.* Washington, U. S. Government Printing Office, 1961.

Academic

Bensberg, Gerald J. (ed.): *Teaching the Mentally Retarded.* Atlanta, SREB Attendant Training Project, 1965.

Davitz, Joel R., Lois J. Davitz, and Irving Lorge: *Terminology and Concepts in Mental Retardation.* New York, Bureau of Publications, Teachers College, Columbia University, 1964.

Dunn, Lloyd M. (ed.): *Exceptional Children in the Schools.* New York, Holt, 1963.

Ellis, Norman R. (ed.): *Handbook of Mental Deficiency.* New York, McGraw-Hill, 1963.

Ellis, Norman R., et al. (eds.): *International Review of Research in Mental Retardation.* New York, Academic Press, 1966.

Johnson, Wendell, Frederic L. Darley, and D. C. Spriestersbach: *Diagnostic Methods in Speech Pathology.* New York, Harper, 1963.

Jordan, Thomas E.: *The Mentally Retarded.* Columbus, Merrill, 1966.

Kirk, Samuel A.: *Educating Exceptional Children.* Boston, Houghton, 1962.

Masland, Richard L., Seymour B. Sarason, and Thomas Gladwin: *Mental Subnormality.* New York: Basic Books, 1958.

Rothstein, Jerome H. (ed.): *Mental Retardation: Readings and Resources.* New York, Holt, 1962.

Stevens, Harvey A. and Rick Heber (eds.): *Mental Retardation: A Review of Research.* Chicago, University of Chicago Press, 1964.

Van Riper, Charles: *Speech Correction Principles and Methods.* New York, Prentice-Hall, 1965.